Boom, Bust and Back Again

Boom, Bust and Back Again

A Property Investor's Survival Guide

Arsh Ellahi

Published by Elite Property Circle
30-32 Chapel Ash
Wolverhampton
WV30TN

BOOM, BUST AND BACK AGAIN

ISBN 978-0-9933315-0-3

Book formatted by www.bookformatting.co.uk.

Contents

Dedication

Dad,

Thank you for all those years of graft, your wise words that I didn't always appreciate at the time, but more importantly thank you for always believing in me.

When I was a boy you were my hero, and as I grew you became my mentor and my best friend.

This book is dedicated to you for making me the person I am today, so I can follow in your footsteps and be a good dad to my darling daughters, Anya and Aila.

You will always be missed

Ahmed Noor Ellahi
1938–2015

Acknowledgements

I would like to express my sincere gratitude to the many people who saw me through this book; to all those who provided support, talked things over, read, wrote, offered comments and assisted in the editing, proofreading and design.

I would like to thank my brother and business partner, Aki. We are complete opposites in character but together we make a great team. I am eternally grateful to my siblings for their commitment and support during the good, the bad and the downright ugly days.

My mother deserves a medal for raising six children with the care and attention she has and the enthusiasm she still shows to this day, Thank you.

My wife, best friend and soul mate Shareen, You keep me grounded, and without you, I wouldn't know what to do. Thank you for believing in me, even when I have the craziest of ideas. Thank you for the love and encouragement you show me every minute of the day.

My beautiful daughters Anya and Aila, I can't wait for you to grow a little older so I can share some of these journeys with you!

My heartfelt thanks to Wasim Rehman for your wise words and honest feedback, it is much appreciated.

Thank you, Peter Jones, for the initial support and to all the property professionals, some who are mentioned in this book, who have influenced and inspired me along my path.

Susie Ellis, you have been a wonderful critical friend throughout the process of writing this book. I greatly appreciate all those long conversations and hours of dedication.

Finally, I would like to take this opportunity to thank all the people who have been on this incredible journey with me. It's been tough but I have loved every high and learnt from the low moments. This is not the end though!

Preface

This book is about how two ordinary men from Wolverhampton took a humble family property portfolio and turned it into a revenue-generating machine.

It wasn't always plain sailing; far from it. There was a period of boom. But as the law of gravity states, 'what goes up must come down', and this was certainly what happened. It *all* came down.

What was remarkable was that in the space of six years they built it all back up and made it better, better than they ever thought possible.

This book is their account of their boom and bust, and how they got it back again.

'If you work hard enough and assert yourself, and use your mind and imagination, you can shape the world to your desires.'

Malcolm Gladwell

Think Positive, Think Property
Lesson 1: Have the right mindset

My name is Arsh Ellahi; I'm thirty-four years old and a property entrepreneur. My brother Aki and I own and manage multiple properties, housing over 500 tenants, and many of these properties are houses in multiple occupation (HMOs). The cash flow from our portfolio allows us to be financially free – a dream at one point I didn't think would ever come true.

I can honestly say that what I do and what I have achieved is not because of an innate talent I have. I am merely the result of a series of lucky breaks. I guess you could call them fortunate coincidences.

The underlying theme of this book is those coincidences. Almost everything we have achieved has been by dealing with the everyday issues that arise and ensuring we take advantage of the opportunities we are presented with. I became a landlord, a letting agent, a franchisor and a public speaker teaching my Local Housing Allowance (LHA) and HMO strategies by doing this. It is sometimes said that the best business models are the ones that are never planned, and this has certainly been true for my business journey.

For example, one of the biggest – if not the biggest – reasons I find myself in the position I am in today is that we discovered a way of managing properties that are let to tenants on benefits. We discovered a way to significantly increase the income far beyond anything most landlords in the social sector could ever imagine.

The same could be said for our letting agency. This now manages over 500 tenancies for our family portfolio as well as our client landlords. This started when we were approached by a local landlord to look after his property. Since then we haven't once advertised for another landlord client, but we have more work than we know what to do with

The same is true of our website ddsmove.co.uk, which is now the leading portal in the benefit market sector. Aki and I devised this purely as a response to a gap we came across in the market, and we saw the potential there. At that time we had no idea just how significant it was to become in the social renting sector.

I firmly believe anyone can be successful. Malcolm Gladwell's *Outliers: The Story of Success* questions what success is and, more importantly, how successful people are made. He says:

> Do you see the consequences of the way we have chosen to think about success? Because we so profoundly personalize success, we miss opportunities to lift others onto the top rung … We are too much in awe of those who succeed and far too dismissive of those who fail. And most of all, we become much too passive. We overlook just how large a role we all play – and by 'we' I mean society – in determining who makes it and who doesn't.

One thing I do know is that my achievements would not have been possible without the right mindset. In my opinion most people who don't achieve their goals don't lack the opportunity to achieve, nor do they lack the skill or expertise to make the most of those opportunities; they simply lack the right mindset. Let me explain.

If you get out there and act on your instinct, an opportunity will present itself. You then have the choice of whether to grab that opportunity or let it pass you by. Over the last few years, experience has taught us never to hold back when an opportunity presents itself. With the right preparation and mindset, we can all benefit just by putting ourselves in a position to receive those opportunities.

Here are the principles I follow that allow me to take advantage of the predicaments I find myself in.

Be positive

What sets the most successful property tycoons apart from the average Joe? They take advantage of every opportunity that comes their way and find a way to make it work, even if they don't know how just yet. A great example is Richard Branson. At the tender age of twenty-eight he bought his own island just six years after starting the Virgin Group. And how is that possible, you may be thinking. Well, in his own words, 'If someone offers you an amazing opportunity but you are not sure how you can do it, say yes and then learn how to do it later!' He spotted a brilliant opportunity and didn't let his lack of business acumen in the aviation field hinder his ability to see the potential to make money.

That's probably why my first reaction to everything is 'Yes I can'. If anybody tells me that I can't do something, I take it as a challenge, and the natural competitor in me strives to demonstrate my ability to do it. If somebody comes to me with a proposition or an opportunity, my initial reaction will be to look at it and to consider how I can make it work and how I can make money out of it. I know that others might be more cautious and think, 'What's the problem and where's the catch?' However, I know my mindset and positive thinking has helped me to grab hold of and enjoy many opportunities. Now I am not implying that you should say yes to absolutely everything – exercising a certain amount of caution is common sense – but what I am saying is that you should be open to opportunities.

Frequently I am asked, 'Do you want to buy my property?' I always say yes. That's always my first reaction. The alternative is to say no, but if I do that they'll just go and find somebody else to buy their property and I'll have missed the opportunity. Someone approached me recently and asked me if I'd like to buy their nineteen-bed HMO for £700,000. I said yes immediately, but then I asked, 'Do you mind if I just do my due diligence on that first?' I haven't closed the door on the deal; I've just said I'm thinking about it. In this case we worked out the numbers and we eventually agreed a 'rent-to-rent' strategy at £90,000 a year.

Believe in Yourself

Having the right mindset begins with dealing with the little chats that you have with yourself in your mind. Now I realise that some people may think that I'm crazy if I talk about 'voices in my head', but this voice is known as your 'inner voice'. It is this inner voice that reflects your self-worth. You are the one that controls that inner speech. You can make it positive or allow it to talk you out of things. If you continually let that inner voice say 'You're not good enough', 'You don't have what it takes to succeed' or 'You're going to mess up', the voice will intrude on your psyche so that the project failing is all you can think about. The starting point for having the right mindset for success is to nip all of those thoughts in the bud and replace them with the 'Yes I can' thoughts, and practise doing this until the negative thoughts don't bother showing up at all. I see so many property investors and potential property investors talk themselves out of doing often excellent deals. If you're constantly telling yourself that you're not going to do the deal, or that you can't afford the deal, or you can't do this or you can't do that, then guess what? You're not going to be able to do it. The only person stopping you from doing it is you.

I think a good example of this is the way people react when they hear that we specialise in renting properties to tenants on benefits. Most weeks I go and speak at property events, where I always pose the question: 'Who here would rent to people on benefits?' Usually a couple of hands go up, but the general consensus is that benefit tenants are a) hard work, and b) not worth the hassle. To me this doesn't make sense because, as far as I'm concerned, they are turning away from a business that is both recession-proof and very profitable. The only thing that differentiates them from me is our respective mindsets. Their mindset has persuaded them to go one way in property whilst my mindset has allowed me to go another way. Although they tell me that I've made the wrong choice, without wanting to sound arrogant, I'm sure that in many cases if we were to compare our financial statements they would speak for themselves.

Have a Plan

You have bought this book for a reason, so I guess you could say you have taken advantage of an opportunity to better yourself and increase your knowledge. You clearly have the drive and ambition to increase your financial gain for a reason that is personal to you, and you are on the path to making changes for the better. Now in order to do well, you have to have a plan. You must know what you want and know how to get there.

This following exercise will require you to reflect on what you want to achieve in life and on your property journey. You may want to take some time to reflect and add to this as you see fit. Remember, this is a working model and should be added to and altered as your journey progresses.

Write down and make a simple plan by drawing four columns on a piece of paper. In the first column write down where you are now. In the second column write down where you want to be. In the third column write the criteria or steps needed to get you there. The final column should be updated to reflect on how well you are doing.

This is a method I use regularly. Below is an example of the plan I made a number of years ago.

I often update and reflect on my current plan at the end of a holiday or a break. The reason for this 'Check point' is that I am refreshed and have had a mental break from my daily work schedule and can therefore reflect on my journey with a clear mind.

What is my current position?	Where do I want to be?	How I am going to get there?	How am I doing?
(Jan 2002) Own 20 properties	'retire' at 45 years old	STAY ALIVE! Look at the time I have available	(Sept 2002)
	Improve portfolio by 100+ properties	What other strategies can I use to maximise cash flow- research and review	Check point
Check point	Look up to inspirational people. How does their journey differ?	This cash flow should allow me to buy more properties	Check point
		Structure loans according to retirement age of 45	Check point

My main goal is to retire when I'm forty-five years old. When I decided that this was what I really wanted in life, I began to arrange things so I could work today with that end goal in mind. The first thing I did was to sit down and think about how I was going to make it happen. I realised that number one on the list is staying alive. I know this might sound like a rather basic requirement for achieving my goal, but it's true. I try not to do anything stupid. In fact, I always put a note in my calendar in big, bold letters – 'Don't do anything stupid!' I know I might come across as a positive, 'nothing's a problem or too much trouble' type of person, but I take risk very seriously. I'm optimistic but I'm not reckless. If something's too risky I'll walk away.

Which leads very nicely to the second thing I realised I needed to do to achieve my goal. If I'm going to retire when I'm forty-five I need to be completely debt free.

After our dreadful experiences in 2008, Aki and I knew that we never wanted to be seriously exposed to debt again, and so we wanted to keep gearing at reasonable levels and make sure the debt gets paid down. Aki and I have learnt not to borrow excessively and to be suspicious of borrowed money. We fully understand why people say that you should gear up as much as you can, but the truth is, when you amass debt you've still got to pay it back one day. If you can't pay it back, there will be consequences. So whenever we take on any property debt now, we always look at how it fits into the long-term picture. We ask ourselves, 'In the long term is it going to help or hinder us?' If we've got available cash we don't take on debt at all, despite the received wisdom that you should always use other people's money if you can. Our philosophy is that we don't want to service a debt when we don't need to. One thing the credit crunch and the subsequent property crash taught us is that there is no guarantee that property prices will always follow an upwards trend, at least not in the short to medium term.

Now all our properties are financed using capital repayment loans rather than interest-only loans. We feel that puts us in control. We are not relying upon market movements to secure the equity within the portfolio. I know this goes against the received wisdom on this subject, but my personal opinion is that an investor should try to repay their debt as quickly as possible.

I recommend that every investor looks at ways of bringing down the debt on their portfolio. I might be looking at this a bit simplistically, but this is how I see it. If you have a portfolio of properties that are worth, say, £1 million and you have borrowing of £750,000, it may well be that in ten years' time the portfolio is worth £2 million, but you will still have borrowing of £750,000. If values don't increase and you are using interest-only loans, then you are no further forward. Following my approach, a portfolio purchased for £1 million may be worth £2 million, but I will have borrowings of zero, which means that my equity is now the full £2 million. Even if values don't increase I've got equity of £1 million and not just £250,000. It's true that I may have paid out a little bit more on the mortgage every month, which will have reduced my cash flow, but I see it as an enforced savings plan that I am putting my money into month after month. This means I know for sure that one day I am actually going to be debt free.

The way I look at it, it's all about risk. The risk of property values not going up may be small, but it exists. By paying down the loans as we go along we know that, no matter what happens, we will always have equity in our portfolio and that equity will be increasing month by month. We have our portfolio structured so that we know all of our loans will be paid down to zero the day before my forty-fifth birthday. On my forth-fifth birthday Aki and I will be completely financially free and I can choose then whether I want to retire or not. My wife is convinced that, like my father, I will never retire. He had an incredibly strong work ethic, and up until the day he was hospitalised with cancer at seventy-six he was still an instrumental part of our business. He continued to maintain the properties, drive his van around to development sites and ensure everything ran smoothly to the high standards he set.

I have a young family, and by the time I'm forty-five my daughters will be teenagers. I want to be a father who is as actively involved as possible.

So, the way I've planned it, regardless of what happens in the market, I am in control of my own destiny. I also realised that to get to my end goal of retiring early I need to keep on doing what I am doing, and to have fun with it.

Be Resilient

According to Wikipedia, resilience is 'the ability to cope with change', and that is certainly something vital in the world of property. It is all about how you cope with change, deal with problems and ultimately pick yourself up after disappointing results. Everything I have experienced throughout my property journey has made me resilient to setbacks, and I do not take no for an answer. As difficult as things can get – and you will read about how difficult things got for us – we are able to cope. This is partly due to my philosophy of working hard to play hard. I definitely try to live life full-on and give a hundred per cent to everything I do. If I try something but it doesn't work out, it doesn't really matter because I know that I have given it everything and I can't do any more than that. I'd be disappointed only if I knew that I hadn't given my all.

Do Not Take No For An Answer

I try not to see problems. It's probably something of a cliché that business and motivation experts talk about, but I've always tried to live by the principle of focusing on finding the solution rather than on the problem.

It might sound naïve, and perhaps even a bit cheesy, but I assume that every problem can be solved; it's just down to how you deal with it.

In the property business there's always going to be some kind of a problem to deal with. It might be that somebody isn't paying their rent, or something needs repairing and it's going to cost me some money. I'm not going to worry about any of that because it can all be resolved. I try not to worry. If a problem comes along I'm going to find a solution. I endeavour to run my office with this theory: don't bring me a problem, bring me a solution.

Have Fun

Having fun is incredibly important to me. If you're not happy I think that means you are doing something wrong, and I think you are less likely to be successful if you aren't happy. Being happy naturally allows you to say yes more often. Being happy and having a positive outlook means that you are less likely to see problems as problems, and consequently you're more likely to deal with them in a constructive way rather than let them drag you down.

The American writer Andy Rooney said, 'Everyone wants to live on top of the mountain, but all the happiness and growth occurs while you're climbing it.' This is how I see things. Some may think this is a rather rose-tinted view of life, but I really think it is important to enjoy what you do. Everybody will have the odd bad day, and I'm no exception. You will read later that we used to spend many Sunday nights fretting about Monday morning, and for good reason. I'm glad to say, we found systems to get around that, as you will see. In any business there are going to be niggles, and in property I find that they're principally with tenants.

It's inevitable that when you're dealing with people, and when you're dealing with money, things will occasionally go awry, but that's just part of the job. Regardless of that, I just love what I do, and I'm sure that's been a big part of my success.

Being happy and enjoying myself doesn't mean that I let myself off lightly. I am a firm believer in hard work, although most of the time it doesn't seem like work because I enjoy doing it so much. I like to keep track of what I'm up to, and I challenge myself regularly. I often ask myself what progress I'm making, and every year I like to look back and ask myself, 'What did you do last year? Have you progressed, and if so how, and how far have you got?' Because of the way that I work, and because of the way that I do things, I do progress year on year, but if I didn't I'd have to ask myself why not. I wouldn't beat myself up, but I would look for the solution to help me to move forward in future, and then I'd make sure I implemented it until my results changed. If you were to ask me what my business goals were I'd say that they are to keep on doing what I'm doing, and to assess every opportunity that comes my way.

I realise that's not the answer most people would expect. Many people would say that their business goal is to be financially free and to make as much money as they can. I suppose the way I see it is that financial freedom and money come naturally when you're happy doing what you're doing.

I have written this book to convince you that everything I am and everything I have done is down to two key factors:

a)   spotting an opportunity and taking it
b)   having a positive mindset

I would like to think this book is a strong resource for people who want to maximise their property potential as well as an interesting read about the journey I have been on.

I'm going to share with you accounts of my life from the last few years, some extremely difficult but most a lesson waiting to be taught. When you see how many things seem to have happened I hope it will encourage and inspire you to get out there and grab some opportunities of your own. I'm not going to show you any get-rich-quick schemes. As with anything worth having in life, the systems and the processes I'll show you require a certain amount of work and effort, so if you are hoping for a quick and easy path to spectacular property income, this probably isn't the book for you. If you are prepared to read it with an open mind, to look at things from a new perspective, and to do a few simple bits of admin, then you will reap the full benefits of the story I am about to tell you.

I firmly believe people in property do not have an innate talent for it. Successful individuals in property are only that way because of a range of choices they have made. They are not born with the talent to source a good deal, but it is something they have established over time, and I believe that with the right tools anyone can make this a profitable business.

'It ain't how hard you hit, it's how hard you can get hit and keep moving forward.'

Rocky Balboa

One Thursday Afternoon

Lesson 2: Do not spend what you do not have

I will never forget that day; it is etched in my memory. One Thursday afternoon late in 2008, Aki, my brother, sat at his desk with his head in his hands. He had just been on the phone appointing an administrator and arranging a time for them to come and collect the files. That was that: the end of the family development business. Bentley Homes had gone under. How different everything had been just a few years before.

Let me explain how the family property development business started and the things that happened that led to that phone call.

The family property development started in a very low-key way. Many years ago my parents had bought a shop, which was actually a couple of terraced houses knocked together. It was very run down; it needed everything doing to it as it had been vacant for a long time. The reason we were so attracted by it was that there was loads of land at the side. Aki and another one of my brothers asked our father if they could do something with the land and he agreed. They set off and got planning permission for a new house on the side plot, and they refurbished the existing building, splitting it back into two houses.

This was back in 1998 when the housing market was recovering after the crash of the early 1990s. When they first thought about taking on this project, they had been aiming to sell for £60,000 to

£65,000 per property, but by the time the work was actually finished they were able to sell them for £90,000 and £95,000.

For a first project it was really exciting. It had given us all a taste for development, and we wanted to do more. With the profit, they bought some land with planning consent for eight houses, but before they had a chance to decide what to do with it they were approached by a company who wanted to build houses for their staff. They had paid about £300,000 and the company was offering them £450,000. An offer they couldn't refuse.

In those days, back before online bank transfers, I remember Aki holding a cheque for £450,000 after the sale had completed. That was a £150,000 profit for doing next to nothing. They were hooked, it was a great feeling and it encouraged them to go out and find more deals. With a rising market they were able to keep ploughing profits back in and buy bigger and bigger plots.

On their next purchase, in 2002, they got planning consent for twenty-two apartments and, although they could have 'flipped' the site on to a developer, they decided to build it themselves. The total costs, including the land and development, were around £2 million, and they sold the apartments for a total of £3.5 million, making a profit of about £1 million over the space of 24 months. The deals were flying in and the feeling of invincibility was contagious.

The development arm of the family business was predominantly led by two of my brothers. My involvement with the main development portfolio was slim. Upon leaving university, I wanted to start a sector of the Ellahi Group independently and so I set up Webuypropertiesfast in 2003, however, we often combined the companies' funds in order to support the purchase and development of projects. Although I played a minimal role in the company, my father had always encouraged the Ellahi brothers to work together and consult each other on deals. So when things were good we all prospered, but when things weren't so positive we shared that responsibility equally.

Up until then my brothers had been trading under the family name of Ellahi Estates, but they thought that if they were going to become fully fledged developers they needed a change of image. So they set up a company called Bentley Homes. It sounded right, it was the image they wanted, and it resonated with quality and luxury.

They continued buying land and the breaks just kept on coming. In 2005, they bought a site with planning consent for eighteen apartments and six houses in a very affluent area of Wolverhampton for £1.35 million. At that time, with the company's track record, they were able to get 100 per cent funding from the bank. Now they were not only doing major deals but they didn't even have to use their own money unless they wanted to. This unspoken power was soon inflating our egos along with our bank balances.

The very next day after the land had been purchased, a large supermarket chain approached them and asked if they would consider selling it.

The supermarket offered £2.55 million just like that. When I heard about the offer I assumed they were winding me up. If somebody rings up and says they are going to offer you big money for a property you've only just bought, you're going to take that proposal very seriously. Having confirmed the authenticity of the offer and obtained proof of funds, the brothers had an in-depth discussion about selling the land to the supermarket or continuing with the original plan to build the development. They knew that in the past a couple of large chains had looked at the site but both had been refused planning permission, so they wanted an unconditional offer before they would agree to sell. The potential buyer was very confident and faxed them an unconditional offer that very afternoon. Just by taking a phone call they made £1.1 million. After rounds of cheering and celebrations in the office we knew Bentley Homes was going from strength to strength and there would be no stopping us.

Bentley Homes had been using a contractor to do the building work, but my brothers thought it would make better business sense to bring everything in-house and become a fully fledged development company. A managing director was employed who had a house-building background, then a land team and a legal team, and in the space of a year Bentley Homes went from having no staff to employing twenty people. My father had always operated as a one-man band and he would often express his concern with the level of overheads Bentley Homes was accumulating.

Within a year of taking the decision to bring the building side in-house they developed a hundred units. We felt like kings; nothing could touch us and we were basking in the boom. For a bunch of lads from Wolverhampton we were really flying, my brothers with Bentley Homes and me with Webuyproperties fast, but things were about to change.

At the beginning of 2008 the company had two large sites on the go: one of about sixty units that was 90 per cent complete and another of forty-five units that was only about 50 per cent complete. They had bought the land for these developments back in 2007 when they had no idea that the credit crunch was coming.

They had been working on a profit margin of around 20 per cent. But as the credit crunch began to unfold, values fell and our margins started to disappear. Valuers were using evidence of forced-sale prices achieved for repossessed properties that had been developed four or five years earlier. At these new lower values they were making a loss on every sale and they needed support from the bank if they were going to complete the development sites and survive.

The directors of Bentley Homes had no choice but to hire an insolvency practitioner to see if he could put a plan together to present to the banks. At that time they were dealing with seven different banks, but unfortunately, although a couple agreed to a rescue package, the others wouldn't. The way development finance worked then was that as the first units on a development sold, the banks held on to the money and wouldn't let you touch a penny until you had paid off their loan.

That's where they came unstuck. As the plots were selling they were paying back the banks, but they had numerous suppliers and contractors who also wanted to be paid. They needed to agree a rescue package with the banks to pay off their suppliers, but by refusing to cooperate the banks also hit the cash flow of all Bentley Homes' suppliers – something that caused them a whole heap of problems.

As you can imagine, morale in the office had hit a low point. They were getting about fifty telephone calls a day from different suppliers wanting to be paid, chasing their money. They had always made sure that the employees were paid, but the staff could work out from the calls that things weren't great and that cash flow was a real problem.

So … on that Thursday afternoon they just had to accept the inevitable. If the banks wouldn't support them, they had no alternative but to appoint administrators and close the business. With that one phone call my brothers effectively said goodbye to £4 million of family money.

At the time of administration, the projects looked like this:

-Project K	42 apartments	(GDV £5m)
-Project S	35 houses & apartments	(GDV£4m)
-Project CC	24 apartments	(GDV £3m)
-Project B	25 houses	(GDV £6m)

Personal Revenue lost		£4m
Credit lost		£10m
Projected Profit Disappeared		£4m

News of the company going into administration made the front page of the local newspaper the following afternoon, and was even repeated on pages four and five for the next few days. Most of the staff left. Only two remained to help tidy things up for the next week or so. They'd both worked with them for many years and they were more like friends than staff. We were incredibly grateful for their support during that difficult time.

Everything we as a family had built up over the previous ten years disappeared overnight. Not just the business but also our lifestyles. We had got used to doing deals bringing in a few hundred thousand pounds profit, and then got used to doing developments bringing in over a million pounds profit. We had also got used to the trappings that go with it – the Porches, the BMWs and the Audis. We had been able to buy whatever we wanted, when we wanted. Then suddenly, one day, there was nothing in the bank and we couldn't squeeze another penny from our credit cards.

A few days after Aki made that fateful phone call, I pulled up outside my mum and dad's house in a six-month-old Audi and the bailiffs were waiting to repossess it. We had no credit facilities with anybody. Anyone who would have given us credit facilities before just didn't want to know us now. We were desperate and down.

My father had always instilled the importance of family support in us, so I put the daily running of my own company to one side and focused on dealing with the aftermath of the demise of Bentley Homes. Now my brothers' problems were my problems too.

The phone call to the administrator wasn't the end of our problems; in some ways it was just the beginning. The bank's decision didn't just affect us. Despite going into administration – the only legal route we could take – our suppliers obviously still wanted to be paid. Other than the unfinished development sites, Bentley Homes had no assets. There was nothing that we or the administrators could liquidate to raise cash to pay our bills. We were just going to have to write everything off. We just couldn't pay the outstanding debts to our suppliers; practically because we had no money, and legally because we were in administration. Unfortunately, they were small businesses who wanted and needed what they were owed, understandably.

One subcontractor to whom we owed about £50,000 got a local gangster, renowned in the West Midlands, to ring our office to tell us that he was collecting the debt and he expected to collect it in full and fast. This gangster had a notorious reputation for causing great harm and we were adamant we wanted to stay in one piece! This was alarming to say the least, and we put even more pressure on the bank to pay us so that we could pay him. Eventually, the bank agreed and we managed to pay up and get the gangster off our backs. We felt relieved, but it wouldn't last. Word got around that if enough pressure was applied we'd pay up. We had another couple of debt collectors come and visit us. One company that was clearly anxious to get their money went to the desperate measure of hiring some local 'heavies' who attempted to solve the situation by threatening to damage our kneecaps in a rather unpleasant manner. They were difficult days, and as low points go, they don't get much lower than that.

Thankfully, about ten years before the demise of Bentley Homes, the family property investment portfolio had been set up as a trust by our family lawyer who felt this was a good policy in the event of something tragic happening, so there was never any prospect that we would lose everything. However, the family business was badly affected because we had used money from that portfolio to build up Bentley, and, of course, all that money was lost along with the rest. We were only able to retain our offices because our other business was named on the lease. Webuypropertiesfast was ok, at least in theory, but we only had access to a limited amount of cash.

The whole Bentley situation was a sobering experience and we vowed that we would never allow ourselves to go through anything like that ever again. It is at times like this that you realise just how much a pound is worth. Overnight we trimmed our costs right down to the point where we would put our coats on rather than turn the thermostat up a few degrees. Every penny we could save on our electricity bill was a penny worth saving.

Going through that dreadful experience totally changed our outlook on money, and brought into focus what we wanted to achieve from life. We made the decision that no matter what it took we were going to get ourselves back into a position of being financially secure again. The most important thing we learnt was not to borrow money beyond our means: if you don't have it, don't spend it.

One of the first things that Aki and I did was to restructure all of the borrowings on the family investments, putting them back onto a repayment basis. We've worked really hard at this. To date, we have paid off around 50 per cent of the debt, which over a six-year period is remarkable to say the least. The way that we've restructured our debt means that we know it will be paid off, and we know to the day how long it is going to take. We decided to get back down to brass tacks, back to our roots, back to basics, and to stick with what we knew worked. It meant starting all over again.

This episode in our lives is called the 'Bust'; it was a time when we experienced and learnt a great deal about the property world. More than anything, it has shaped the way we do business today and we vowed never to make those mistakes again. Unfortunately, the failure of Bentley Homes didn't just affect the family financially; it also affected our sibling relationships. The two brothers who spearheaded the company decided to go their separate ways. One brother chose to stay and work alongside me to revive the business, while the other decided he wanted a break after this extremely distressing period in his life, and chose to move on.

Upon reflection, Bentley Homes made a series of errors that ultimately led to its collapse. To avoid similar mistakes, when you are making property decisions make sure you consider:

1   **Funding** – Do you have sufficient funds available to redeem any loans?

2.   **Exit strategy** – What is your exit strategy?

a)   To sell the properties – is there sufficient evidence to back up your values?

b)   To re-finance the properties – How will they be valued?

c)   To let the properties – Is there sufficient demand?

'The only person you are destined to become is the person you decide to be.'

Ralph Waldo Emerson

'Drop Me Somewhere Nice'

Lesson 3: Make the most of every opportunity

Like many men of his generation my father came over from Pakistan in the early 1960s, I suppose you could say to seek his fame and fortune. He arrived at Heathrow one drab and dreary November afternoon with just £3 in his pocket. Jumping into the first taxi cab on the rank he said, 'Drop me somewhere nice.'

I guess we all have different ideas of 'nice' as after a few hours of driving he was dropped in Wolverhampton! The cab driver took £2 of his £3, so in unfamiliar surroundings, and with just £1 in his pocket, my father started the challenge of rebuilding his life. He had left behind a partially sighted father along with siblings to support, and coming to the UK in the 60s was his way of fulfilling that responsibility.

He wasn't without qualifications; he was an educated man, a fully trained and skilled precision engineer, and he secured a job with an engineering company. Over those first few years he worked for a number of companies, and slowly but surely he saved his wages every month until he was eventually able to buy his own factory. This was something he was very disciplined about. No matter what, every month he would split his salary in three, with one third covering his living expenses, one third sent back to his mum in Pakistan, and the last third put aside in his savings account. Those savings allowed him to buy an industrial unit from which he ran his own engineering company. He was a skilled engineer and good at what he did, so he landed large contracts with companies like Caterpillar and the LEX Group. As the engineering business prospered he was able to diversify his savings into more property, and eventually he owned a small portfolio.

Engineering was his first love, and as a child I always thought that I was going to be an engineer as well because I'd spend every evening, or so it seems looking back, helping dad in the business. This started when I was four years old; whilst other kids were playing football or going to the park, I was helping my dad. I was there on Saturdays, Sundays, school holidays, you name it, my dad had me and my brothers working there. Curiously for a small child, I didn't mind at all, in fact I really quite enjoyed it. Even at that young age I had the expectation that this was going to be my life, that engineering and working in the family business were going to be my destiny.

Property was never going to be a full-time business for my father as he was too busy with his main business, but it was actually my mother and an unfortunate incident that started the property empire.

It's an old cliché that behind every good man is an even better woman, and this was certainly the reason the property business became such a huge part of our lives. When my mother arrived from Pakistan at the age of twenty-one, she was a homely woman who wanted to do as much as she could to be the best wife to my father. So after dividing up the chores in the house, my father informed her that it was her task to do the weekly grocery shopping. He took her to the market in town and showed her where she could obtain all the household and weekly goods. She was determined to do a fantastic job for her new husband. The following week, my father gave her his hard-earned £5 and sent her on her way. She shopped like there was no tomorrow and she bought all the necessary items for the month. Extremely pleased with herself, she arrived home. Later that evening, my father asked how much change she had from her £5 note. 'None,' she replied with an eager grin on her face. 'I spent it all!' My father's face dropped, and with all the patience he could muster he informed her that he got paid £7 per week and out of that he needed to pay all the bills, put petrol in the car and save some money. She was horrified at the consequences of her actions and vowed she would do what she could to help him make money. She noticed that each week the man they rented their spare room to paid them £2. She realised this was an opportunity in the making. 'This is great,' she thought, 'we don't have to do anything and he just comes and hands us £2 each week!' So she spoke to my father and encouraged him to rent out the other spare room in their house. Every week she diligently saved those £2s, and with that the property business started to grow.

With the money they saved, my father bought mainly three-storey mid-terraced properties. They were all in Wolverhampton, within a ten-minute drive of where we lived. He loved to tell me that the most he ever spent on a property was £2,500, but £2,500 was a lot of money back then.

As the portfolio grew, so did the need for a system of managing it. The need to be able to communicate with people was essential, so my mother asked some of the tenants to teach her English so she could take the strain off my father and deal with the tenants. She had a clever way of making tenants pay rent by coming to the back door connected to the kitchen to give her their rent. She cooked, looked after us and managed the tenants at the same time, all from her kitchen-come-office. Soon enough, she was making calls to the council along with dealing with any issues the tenants had, which also made her the local social worker. Needless to say, my parents made a great team. Although a woman of many talents, the one skill my mother failed to acquire was the ability to drive. After a number of attempts, she finally came to terms with this and I became the newest and youngest driver in the household.

By the time I was seventeen and had learnt to drive, I was sent out as a part-time sales rep for the engineering business. I'd go and see clients like Caterpillar and ask if they had any more work that needed doing, but by 1997 many of our clients were sending work abroad because it was cheaper for them, and business started to slow down. Inevitably, the writing was on the wall for the family engineering business.

After my A-levels, I studied international business management with international market management at the University of Gloucestershire. When I graduated there was an expectation that I would go back into the family business, but by that time I didn't really fancy it. My father was getting quite elderly and was expecting me to take over a lot of his activities. The problem was that he'd always been very hands-on and I could see that any role I took on at the factory would be labour intensive. I thought there must be easier ways to make money, so I persuaded him that my energies would be better spent looking after his property portfolio. He agreed to pay me £100 a week. My father was paying me less than the minimum wage and expecting me to work a fifty-hour week! Upon reflection, he had a method to his madness. He paid me a very basic wage to start with so I would work hard to prove myself; just because I was his son didn't mean I would get an easy ride.

My first self-appointed task was to review the portfolio – how it was performing, how it was run – and try to identify any areas where it could be improved. He had about twenty properties, and by today's standards that wouldn't be seen as a large portfolio, but back in his day my dad was quite innovative because not that many people were investing in property. In the 1960s and 1970s, property investing was really the preserve of the rich or of small property companies. By the time I'd left university, property investing was becoming more popular, but even then buy-to-let was still in its early days.

Most of my dad's properties were houses let to single families, but he did have a few HMOs. Again, I consider that to be quite innovative because HMOs weren't as popular or, dare I say, as trendy as they are today. They were considered a bit *Rising Damp*, and were hard to finance and generally thought to be hard to manage. My dad, being a natural businessman, didn't see it that way; he thought having multiple occupancies was a good way to lower his risks. He took the view that if one tenant moved out he'd only have an empty room rather than an empty property.

He learnt all this from personal experience. When he moved from Pakistan to England he lived with one of his engineering colleagues because he couldn't afford to rent a whole property for himself. His friend only rented him a room. So my father, knowing no different, thought that was just the way things were done in England; you didn't occupy a whole property, you just occupied one room. When he eventually bought his first house in 1973, he moved my mum and, when we were born, all six children into the ground floor, and let the first floor out as individual bedsits, with some prompting from my mum. From an early age I noticed that we never occupied a whole house. As his investment portfolio increased, that was the model he continued to follow. Where he could, he let houses as individual rooms because he knew it offered much more income security than letting individual houses to single families.

The seeds were sown; by looking after my father's portfolio I stumbled across the system that would eventually allow me to significantly increase returns across the board.

'I am not a product of my circumstances. I am a product of my decisions.'

Stephen Covey

15% or 100% Risk?

Lesson 4: Review your portfolio in terms of risk

Having graduated from university, and managing to side-step the pressure to join the family engineering business, in 2003 I found myself reviewing my dad's property portfolio. He had a mix of working tenants, professionals, and tenants on benefits. Going through the figures, and auditing the rents, I was surprised to see that most rent defaults were by the working and professional tenants. I could also see that the working tenants paid their rent a month in arrears, which struck me as not that great for cash flow. In fairness, my dad was too busy in the engineering business to fully appreciate what was happening with the properties, and he was convinced that having professional and working tenants was good for the portfolio. The more I looked into it, the more I realised that wasn't the case. At the end of every month at least one working tenant would take off, doing a moonlight flit. There's always somebody who will try to take advantage, and that was a temptation too far for many of our tenants. After all, it was very easy for them. Because they were paying a month in arrears, they used the room for a month and then they paid their rent. So at the end of the month some would think to themselves, 'Now I've had a month rent free, I'm going to do a runner.' It's funny how we all see things differently; my father remained convinced that having working tenants paying rent in arrears was still the best way to run a property portfolio.

Despite what he thought, the figures didn't lie. As I looked at them I could see that the situation was completely different for those tenants who were on benefits. The council paid their rent, and they paid it direct to my father. The only issue I saw was that there was a lot more administration work to be done filling out forms and chasing housing benefit claims. There were no arrears, no problems, and no bad debts. Every four weeks we received a schedule from the council telling us who the tenant was, which property they occupied, how much they had been paid and the period they had been paid for. It was really straightforward, and I thought that this was just a brilliant system.

I guess I've always thought a little bit differently to other property investors. Instead of looking at the figures in terms of income, I started to look at them in terms of risk. Let me explain what I mean. I could see that 100 per cent of the rent due from a working or professional tenant was payable by the tenant, so if they didn't pay we lost all of their rent. It was different with the tenants claiming benefits because most of their rent was paid by the council. For example, suppose the rent was £100 per week for a particular tenant. The council would pay £85 and the tenant would pay a top-up of £15 to make up the shortfall. It didn't take a genius to work out that if the tenant didn't pay we'd only lose 15 per cent instead of the full 100 per cent. The council guaranteed £85 a week, so it was completely risk free. From a business point of view, it made perfect sense to me to try to fill the rooms with as many tenants on benefits as we could find.

There's a perception in the property investment world that having tenants on benefits is troublesome, that benefit claimants aren't nice people, or that they don't respect the property. I acknowledge that some tenants aren't the most desirable characters, but my father always taught me to give people a chance and show everyone respect regardless of what they can or can't do for you.

Having reviewed my father's books and discovered that we were losing more money from our working tenants than from our tenants on benefits, I introduced a policy whereby when a professional or working tenant left a property we replaced them with a tenant on benefits. It's funny, but my dad was never convinced by this strategy. He said, 'I think you're crazy. Just don't make me bankrupt!' I think he was sceptical because he thought that we were putting all our eggs in one basket, but I saw it as a way of minimising our risk because suddenly, overnight, 85 per cent of our rent was now risk free. Think about it this way: when you have a working tenant there's always a chance they could lose their job, and it would be more than likely they would default on their rent. Ironically, they could end up claiming benefits anyway. For me, personally, as well as the relief that the income stream was now more secure, it meant that I didn't have to go chasing tenants at the end of each month for their rent because I knew that it was going to pop automatically into our bank account. In fact, the amount of income we were collecting increased so much that we were able to be far more relaxed about the top-ups, and I have to confess that quite often we didn't collect them or chase them. It got to the point where we saw collecting the top-up as a bonus, and we ran the business on the basis that we were collecting the 85 per cent from the council.

Slowly but surely, all the tenants in my father's portfolio were on benefits and we became specialists in this niche sector of the market. We systemised the business and streamlined it as much as possible to make things run smoothly. We had systems to get benefits tenants into the properties. We knew exactly when, how, where and how much they were going to get paid, and with this information we approached the local authority. We went out of our way to develop excellent relationships with the local authorities and we became recognised as one of the leading providers of social housing in our area. We were on first-name terms with many of the local authority officers and had a great rapport with them, and over time we got everything working really well.

In 2008, the way that housing benefit was calculated and paid changed when the LHA was introduced. By then we had had several years during which the portfolio was very secure, everything was systemised and it was all plain sailing. I suppose it's inevitable that when things are that good they're not going to stay that way forever.

If you are sceptical about renting to people on benefits, have a look at the following pros and cons.

Pros	Cons
Secure method of rent High demand for properties Less risk of debt Longer tenancies Fewer voids Easy to systemise	Possibly harder to manage Cause more wear and tear to properties

'First, have a definite, clear practical ideal; a goal, an objective. Second, have the necessary means to achieve your ends; wisdom, money, materials, and methods. Third, adjust all your means to that end.'

Aristotle

The Green Cheques

Lesson 5: A business must be systemised in order to run smoothly

In 2008 the government changed the way that housing benefit was dealt with, and everything we had worked so hard to build up began to rock a little. This was actually quite a difficult time for us because it undermined some of the certainties I'd been relying on, particularly when it came to the payment and receipt of rent. As so often happens, although it was extremely inconvenient in the short term, we were able to adapt to the changes and unexpectedly it turned out that they provided a major opportunity, which later led to us forming and running a whole new business.

There was a whole journey we had to go through to get there though. The practical effect of the LHA was to abolish the old housing benefit system for all new tenants on benefits. The rent went from being paid direct to the landlord to being paid direct to the tenant.

This provided quite a challenge as you can imagine. LHA is paid to the tenant fortnightly so there is always the risk that two payments a month could go missing if the tenants decide not to pass them on. Even worse, it was quite common, when a tenant put in a benefit claim, for it to take weeks and weeks for the local authority to process it, meaning that a tenant could occupy the property for, say, ten weeks and then suddenly be presented with ten weeks' worth of rent. For some people it felt like Christmas had come early and the temptation to spend was too much for them. Well, we all know what's going to happen next; they're going to do a moonlight flit with the cheque and that will be that. Unless you took rent in advance and had a deposit guarantor, landlords were left very vulnerable to tenants who were in a position to hurt them financially. Unfortunately, that has happened on many occasions. Overnight we'd gone from having an almost totally risk-free income, backed, guaranteed and paid for by the council, to having a totally at-risk income where collection was hit and miss. Suddenly, years of deliberately developing and nurturing a portfolio of tenants on benefits seemed futile, and I wondered if we were now in a worse position than if we'd continued to take working tenants. I couldn't help thinking about my dad's scepticism, and his plea not to bankrupt him. But as I often say, and as I will no doubt say again, I don't like to let a challenge get the better of me, and so I had a long, hard think about what we could do to bring things back onto an even keel. Whenever you are presented with a problem, think about it, take some time away from it, and then make a list of all the possible solutions. Most importantly, do not let it overcome you.

The solution we devised was to approach the council in Wolverhampton and ask them to pay any new tenants claiming benefits with a cheque. At first the local authority seemed quite reluctant. After all, as they pointed out, under the new LHA rules we could apply for direct payment again, but only after the tenant was at least eight weeks in arrears. We weren't prepared to allow them to get eight weeks into arrears before we received direct payment because we knew that would hit our cash flow very severely. After a little bit of to-ing and fro-ing, Wolverhampton council agreed that they would pay our tenants direct with a cheque. This sat in line with the regulation that they should pay the tenant direct. We knew payment was made every other Monday, so we put together a list of tenants who would be receiving a cheque, and their addresses. On those Monday mornings, we would go and see the tenants in the hope we would arrive at a similar time to the postman so when the cheque was delivered we were there to collect the money owed to us.

It was like Formula One Monday. We drove from property to property with the crazy situation of us arriving just in time to spot the postman doing his rounds, whilst inside, unbeknown to us, the tenant would be crouched down by the letterbox, also waiting for the postman. As soon as the cheque arrived, they'd grab the envelope, be out of the back door, through the garden, over the fence and on their way to the cheque-cashing shop while we were just knocking on the front door. I am sure there are some Olympic athletes out there who would have had a less gruelling training schedule. Human beings are nothing if not ingenious, and some of our tenants became very ingenious indeed. Unfortunately the result was that our cash flow was being hit and we were losing money, again.

You might be wondering how that helped us. After all, if the cheque is made out in the tenant's name then we couldn't cash it anyway. We also thought that a cheque was an obstacle for the tenant as it would take three to five days to clear if they banked it. Usually that is true, but at the same time as we approached Wolverhampton council to ask them to pay our tenants by cheque, we'd also been to our bank and made special arrangements so that when the tenant signed the back of the cheque we could cash it. This is called third-party indemnity. In fact, as far as I'm aware, we were the first landlord in the country to make use of this arrangement. We would hand the tenant a pen and ask them to sign the cheque, take it to the bank and pay it into our account. Job done … or so we thought.

For the first few weeks the system worked just fine, but it didn't take long for some of the tenants to realise that they were missing a trick. All that money was in and out of their grasp within seconds. The temptation must have been preying on their minds because after a few weeks some of the tenants stopped opening their doors to us, and as the cheque was in their name they could go to any cheque-cashing centre, cash it and spend the money before we could do anything about it.

We'd be in the office worrying about how much money we'd lose that week; it became very stressful and it got to the point where we were finding it difficult to sleep on a Sunday night, wondering what was going to happen on Monday. We also had problems during holidays and festive periods. For example, tenants were paid on a Monday, but if it was a bank holiday, Christmas or Easter, the cheques would be sent out earlier, but we weren't entirely sure when they were going to hit the doormats. Christmas is one of the worst times of the year for a tenant to be tempted to cash a cheque and not pass over the rent. So despite our best endeavours, and despite our initial success, we had to think of yet another way of doing things.

Back to the drawing board. This is what we came up with. We approached all of the major high-street banks and asked them if they would create accounts for our tenants but give us third-party control. It was an audacious plan and, perhaps not surprisingly, most said no. One, though, with whom we had a very good working relationship, agreed to a trial run with thirty of our tenants. When a new tenant came in, before they signed any housing benefit forms they would go with us to the bank and open up a bank account in their name specifically to receive their LHA. One of the terms of our tenancy agreement gave us third-party access to that account. So every other Monday morning, the LHA would be paid direct into the tenant's bank account, and we could sit in our office and log on to the banking system via the internet and access their account. That meant that we could pay it straight over into our bank account. Everything was under control again.

No more driving around madly, no more tenants jumping over the back garden fence. Everything was as it should be and we were receiving our rent again, hassle free. To this day, I still think this is the best system we have ever devised. Have you noticed, though, how life doesn't let you rest on your laurels too long? At the point where we had our first thirty accounts up and running, a new regional manager was appointed by the bank who didn't know us well and was unconvinced by our motives. I assume that without the previous relationship, and without him understanding the reasons we had set up the system, it all looked a bit suspect to him. We managed to settle on a limit of thirty accounts, and so as far as new tenants were concerned we were back to square one.

Don't get me wrong, having thirty tenants on the system was helpful, but to put this into perspective, by that time Aki and I had been building our own portfolio and, together with my father's portfolio, we had 200 tenants. That meant that we had 170 tenants who weren't signed up to the system and whose rent payments were potentially hit and miss. I'd estimate that around 10 to 15 per cent of our rent was going missing, and there was very little we could do about it. We knew the tenants were getting the cheques, but this wasn't what we were being told. 'Arsh,' they would say, 'we haven't had a cheque yet.' But when I called up the council asking if they'd sent the cheque out I'd be told, 'Yes, we posted it out on Wednesday and it's already showing as being presented.' Meaning that the cheque had been cashed and the money spent.

At that stage there was nothing the local authority could or would do about it. There was nothing we could do either except contact the tenant and make an arrangement for them to catch up on their rent and then start the process of eviction if they wouldn't. This situation was very frustrating because we thought there must be a better way to collect the LHA, if only we knew what it was. As it turned out, the solution to this issue would come as the result of another lucky coincidence.

We were still waiting to find a system that allowed us to double our rent and triple our income, which would make LHA so much more attractive again. Once we discovered that the rent cheque had been presented we'd call the tenant into our office and email the council straightaway requesting that they stop all further cheques going out to the tenant, and we'd get their benefit claims suspended. We also requested direct payment so the rent came straight to us. The local authority would write to the tenant asking if they had paid the rent, and we would send in rent statements and other evidence showing that they hadn't. Sometimes, at this point the tenant would run away. When you find yourself in this situation you realise that you're acting on your own because the local authority are not really empowered to do anything to help you. Having paid the tenants, the council did little to help us and didn't have jurisdiction in this area as their concern was paying the tenant, not controlling how they spent their money. As you can imagine, this was highly frustrating for us landlords. As far as the council were concerned, it was up to the tenant how they used the money and whether they wished to pay the landlord rent or not.

LHA was introduced as part of the government's desire to 'educate' claimants on benefits and to help them learn to be 'financially responsible' and to budget. I agree with that to an extent, but, being a landlord, rent should be an essential priority and paid with immediate effect. Occasionally, I have tenants in my office who present me with what they feel are good grounds, at least from their perspective, for not paying the rent that fortnight. I have heard the 'It's my child's birthday', 'It's Christmas', 'I've had an unexpected problem' and 'It's been a tough month' arguments, and in most cases I try to help them out when I can, following my parents' example. We'd ask them to pay an extra £10 a fortnight until they'd caught up again. This could take a while, but over the years we've recovered a lot of bad debt doing this. This way we are able to keep the tenant and not have a void when the property isn't producing rent. But please be warned, letting tenants amass a large amount of debt is not advisable as they will most likely struggle to pay it back and turn to undesirable means of repayment. I would advise against it unless you have known the tenant well for a long time and haven't experienced other problems with them.

By that time, we were also wise to the need to take a deposit up front whenever we could. It's not always possible with tenants on benefits, but if a tenant had paid a deposit and then done a runner, at least we had the deposit, which gave us some comfort along with a month to get the property let and cash flowing again. Even so, we still had to go through the whole rigmarole of finding a new tenant, helping them make their claim, waiting for their first cheque to go in and generally making sure things were in order and running smoothly. It really began to feel like hard work, especially after having done it several hundred times.

My philosophy is that if something is stressful and you cannot find a solution, you're not doing it properly, so we were looking for another system we could use that would alleviate all the hassle.

What we needed was a system like the one we'd arranged with our bank by which the LHA could be paid into a bank account over which we had part control, or at least some influence. If the banks wouldn't provide this we'd have to look elsewhere. In our quest to create the perfect system we approached a credit union and asked if they would assist us. Credit unions are financial institutions democratically controlled by their members, and operated for the purpose of promoting thrift, providing credit at competitive rates, and providing other financial services to their members, so from our perspective the attraction of working with them is that they can provide what is effectively a bank account for those who either can't, or won't, open a regular account. Even in this day and age many benefits claimants don't have a bank account, often because they don't 'fit' the bank's criteria. Commercially speaking, there's little incentive for a bank to help them or have them as a customer.

We could then tell the tenant to instruct the credit union to 'ring-fence' the LHA payments and set up the equivalent of a direct debit, payable to us. I have to confess that we were somewhat surprised at the initial reluctance of this banking service provider to help us. Their immediate response was that they didn't want to open accounts for all of our tenants on the basis that they would see the money come in and then go straight back out again when it was paid over to us. They couldn't see how they were going to make any money themselves or benefit from the process. We invited them to quote a fee for the service and they came back with a ridiculous figure like £10 per tenant per transaction, which we thought was preposterous. But after a bit of haggling we eventually agreed on £5 per payment per tenant.

We tend to fall into things by chance just by trying to resolve a problem, but, without knowing it at the time, we were again being innovative, as I later found out that we were the first landlords to deal with this problem in this way. While it's true that credit unions operate nationwide, for whatever reason they had not yet reached the Wolverhampton area.

This is the way it would work. We would advertise for, and find, a tenant and, if everything checked out, at the point they signed their tenancy agreement they would also agree to open an account with the banking facility. By that time we'd also have helped them make their application for LHA with a request to the local authority that their money was to be paid straight to the credit union account in their name. Once the LHA payment was received, it would be ring-fenced and sent to us every twenty-eight days. They would also send us a spreadsheet showing the name of the tenant, where they lived and how much money we'd been sent on their behalf. It was almost like the pre-2008 days when we used to receive our money direct from Wolverhampton council, and they'd send us the spreadsheet showing the amounts paid and for whom. The only information missing was the period for which the payment had been made, but we knew it was for the previous four weeks. By using this system, we automatically started to get back on top of the payments and protect our cash flow, but we also discovered an unexpected opportunity.

According to housing benefit regulation, if a tenant had been overpaid for whatever reason, the rules stated that the local authority must recover this overpaid money from the recipient. If the landlord had been paid directly, the authority could claim back the overpayment from them. There were exceptions to this rule. If the tenant had personal issues the landlord was unaware of, the landlord could appeal and argue that the money should be recovered from the tenant.

Overpayments are particularly frustrating when you, as the landlord, are completely unaware that the tenant shouldn't be receiving LHA and you take it in good faith, only to have to pay it back, sometimes many months later. In some cases, the tenant would have vacated the property months earlier. That can feel like a real kick in the teeth and is obviously yet another thing that can hurt your cash flow.

The local authority would recover the money from the tenant in small instalments to ensure they were not financially distressed by it. In Wolverhampton the most they could recover from a tenant was £10.65 per week, which was taken out of their housing benefit going forward. This resulted in us having to reconfigure our systems when tenants applied for one of our properties, as we would investigate if they had any overpayment issues and calculate their housing benefit claim based on this.

Using this strategy wasn't the final step in the evolution of our high-cash-flow LHA system but it was an important one. It was through our understanding and use of this system that we were able to take the concept to a whole new level to produce something that will truly benefit any landlord, anywhere in the country, who has tenants on benefits.

I realise that as I tell the story you might be thinking, 'Arsh, you should have listened to your dad, and should only have taken working tenants. It all sounds like too much hard work.' The truth is, even with all of these periodic problems and setbacks, it still made perfect financial sense for us to be in the benefits market. Just think about this.

Back then the three-bedroom rate for LHA was probably around £120 a week, which is the equivalent of £520 per month. If we were to rent the same property to a working tenant the market rent would probably have only been around £420 to £450 a month. So even with the risk that the rent may prove harder to collect from time to time, we were still getting about 25 per cent over and above what we'd collect from working tenants.

Investors and property specialists regard the benefits market as a tough market, but if you weigh up the advantages of benefits tenants over working tenants, you will soon realise it can be more lucrative. However, what I have come to realise is that to manage benefits tenants effectively, you have to have the correct approach and skill set when dealing with them.

When a new tenant approaches me, I have a set of guidelines I employ to evaluate whether they are the right sort of tenant for me. When vetting a new benefits tenant, do the following:

1. **Take a reference from a previous landlord**
   Always be a little wary if the landlord gives them an absolutely glowing reference – are they trying to get rid of them? Ask about rent arrears, any issues that arose and how they treated the property.

2. **Check their housing benefit history**
   Providing the tenant has tenant has previously lived in the same borough, with the tenant's consent you can call the housing benefit department and check their history.

3 **Check their bank statements**
   You can ask to see a copy of the tenant's bank statement to see if they are financially fixed to pay

your rent or top-up. Check if they are continually overdrawn and what direct debits they have going out every month.

4. **Inspect their current property**
    Ask to go and view the property they are vacating. Do it straightaway so the tenant does not have the opportunity to clean up or cover up any issues.

5   **Use your sixth sense**
    If their current residence is too far away you will have to rely on your gut instinct. If they have arrived in a vehicle, consider the condition of the interiors; this will be a good indicator of the way they will treat your property.

6   **Have a chat**
    Have a ten-minute chat with them and ask them why they want to move and live in your property. Their response will provide you with an insight into their position, and if there are any alarm bells you will soon hear them ringing. It is during this chat I ask the tenant if they have had any issues with the police and what they were. Encouraging them to be open and frank about this is vital if you want to avoid criminal activity in your property.
    In some situations, bad landlords push their tenants into difficult positions. Below is an example of how a rogue landlord treated their tenant, and as a result the tenant exercised her right to withhold rent.

I was approached by a tenant who disclosed that she owed her current landlord £6,000 in rent arrears. A landlord's immediate reaction would be to quickly end the conversation and not give her a chance. But I asked why this happened and she went on to explain that the landlord had refused to carry out any maintenance to the property and her family (including her young children) had been left with no hot water or heating for over a year. As a result, the tenant had contacted the council and requested that her housing benefit be withheld until the work had been completed. What this told me was that the tenant had not simply spent this benefit money but enforced her rights as she did not feel the property was habitable. I checked with the council and they confirmed this and all was in order. Upon inspection of the property, I agreed it was not to an acceptable standard and agreed to take the family on. Four years on and they have not missed a payment and continue to maintain the property to a high standard.

'The person who says it cannot be done should not interrupt the person who is doing it.'

Chinese proverb

Nothing like A Flipping Good Deal

Lesson 6: Short-term property deals can generate cash quickly

'Flipping' is an investment strategy in which an investor buys discounted properties with the goal of reselling them for a profit. The profit can be generated by either price appreciation or as a result of renovation and capital improvements.

When I started Webuypropertiesfast (WBPF) in 2003 it was for the purpose of generating some cash flow for the group of companies, as the development company was starting to expand and needed further capital. There was nothing particularly innovative about WBPF. It was simply a company that purchased properties from homeowners or investors who were after a quick sale. In exchange for a speedy, efficient and guaranteed sale, we required a discount in price. This would ordinarily be between 15 and 30 per cent below the current market value.

The company did exactly what it said on the tin – we bought properties fast. We just advertised in the local paper saying that we would buy properties for cash quickly. It was a simple approach that a lot of investors have used. It might be simple but it works, and we got a lot of leads. Our primary strategy then wasn't to do anything fancy; we just bought the properties cheaply for cash and then we put them back up for auction and sold them on at a profit. As the business grew we started getting more and more leads, so if we found that we didn't have enough cash to do all the deals that month, there were a couple of other strategies we discovered we could also use.

We could take control of the property using an option. An option is a legal agreement that gives the option holder the right to purchase a property at an agreed price within an agreed timeframe. It doesn't impose an obligation to buy the property, but once the option agreement is signed the vendor can't sell the property without the buyer's consent. It gives the purchaser an exclusivity period of between thirty and sixty days to complete the deal. What we'd usually do was agree with the vendor that we could put the property up for auction and sell it on. Once we got the price we were after we could exercise the option, pay the vendor the price they wanted and complete with our purchaser.

An alternative strategy was to exchange on the property but delay completion indefinitely so we could put it up for auction. If and when it sold at auction we could then complete simultaneously with the buyer and the seller.

Using these strategies meant that we didn't have to tie up all of our cash, although buying outright for cash was still our preferred strategy as it was quick and simple and gave us ultimate control of the property. Buying with cash meant we weren't spending beyond our means – a lesson learnt from the events of 2008. This is a simplified model of flipping properties:

A rather exasperated landlord who was tired of all the grief and hassle that being a landlord can bring approached me as he wanted to sell his property. He was offering a three-storey, mid-terraced house in Wolverhampton that he had split and converted into three self-contained flats, but he had never obtained planning permission.

He also had all the tenancies set up so that the rents were inclusive of all bills. The landlord was not making any money from the property as the bills were extremely high due to lack of care by the tenants. People are more likely to turn lights off and turn the heating down if they have to pay for it themselves. Not surprisingly the cash flow from this property was poor and this landlord felt that he had to endure a lot of grief to make not very much money.

We undertook our research and came to the conclusion that the property was probably worth around £90,000, but with a bit of negotiating we eventually managed to buy it for £70,000.

It was only producing around £7,000 a year in rent, which for three flats we felt was very low.

As soon as we completed the purchase, I arranged to meet the current tenants and explained the fact that the rent was extremely low and the all-inclusive contract was not viable for us any longer. I clarified the situation and informed them that I wanted to keep them on as tenants, however, I would require some co-operation from them as they were not currently claiming their full housing benefit because the rent was so low.

With a bit of strategic planning and administration, we were able to more than double the rental value.

As soon as the new tenancies were in place and we could prove the higher rental income, we put the property up for auction and it sold to an investor for £135,000.

So in the space of a few months we made a profit of £65,000 by following some of the rules of flipping.

This profitable deal was completed following a number of Principles you should consider if you are looking to flip properties:

- Look for the potential in a deal
- There may be an uplift that will create a new market value for the property
- Maximise rental income where possible in order to increase the investment/market value
- Structure tenancy agreements so that the tenant deals with all bills (I run a course that specifically deals with this issue. See arshellahi.com for further information)
- Ensure you have an exit strategy
- What is your plan B if your exit strategy doesn't happen? Can you retain the property long term?
- If you do not have an exit strategy, how will this investment sit in your portfolio?

If the property above had not sold at auction, on the basis that I purchased it for £70,000 and it was now producing £15,000 per annum, I would have been producing a yield of 21 per cent, which is unheard of in the UK.

When Webuypropertiesfast was actively trading, prior to 2006, I was approached by the owners of two houses who were fed up of maintaining their gardens, which were far too large for the properties. The owners decided to try to sell them as a potential development plot. We appraised the opportunity and saw that it could potentially be very profitable. We thought this was an interesting idea as at that time local authorities were in favour of infill development because of the shortage of houses.

The vendors were very eager to complete, and we had to do a deal within seven days. The financials looked like this:

Purchase gardens:	£25,000 x 2 = £50,000
Legal costs:	£1,000
Architect fees:	£2,000
Total cost:	£53,000

The property field has a reputation for being a gold mine waiting to be discovered by the next person who delves into it, however, many people who are new to the industry find inexperience and lack of knowledge cost them dearly. I've made many mistakes and have learnt many lessons from the hiccups and issues I have experienced, but the difference is I always pick myself up, take note and vow never to do it again, especially if it has had a financial impact. It's fair to say I've been hit a few times, but I continue to bounce back as a smarter business person.

Having spent £53,000, we were aiming to get planning permission to put a pair of semi-detached houses on the site, each valued at £180,000, and sell the plot at auction. We calculated that each garden was worth £60,000 as a building plot, or £120,000 for the pair, so we got a fantastic deal.

Even if we achieved £100,000 we would still come out with a decent profit of £47,000 for very little work.

I knew that planning permission for a bungalow on the plot had been refused, but dismissed this as we were putting forward a completely different scheme (two-storey semi-detached houses), which would also benefit the area.

We completed on the deal and immediately applied for planning permission. We quickly came up against some opposition. Believe it or not, it was the people who sold us the land who opposed the plans. But this was not the real issue.

As we pushed the deal through quickly we didn't do the normal amount of due diligence, which was an error on my part. The planners also wanted to see an ecological survey for the site as there were badgers there, which we were unaware of. The survey cost £3,000.

We had to jump through all the hoops and were still refused planning permission. We had further consultations with planning officers and even employed a planning consultant as it was proving harder than expected to get the permission. The application went to appeal and failed again, with another rejection against the property.

The consultancy fee was a further £3,000, meaning the plot had now cost us £59,000.

Eventually I decided to cut my losses and I sold the land at auction with the indicative drawings,

Eventually I decided to cut my losses and I sold the land at auction with the indicative drawings, showing a prospective purchaser what it could accommodate (subject to planning). We put an extremely low guide price on it to generate interest. From memory, bidding started at £8,000 and eventually reached £28,000.

After auction costs and legal fees we got back £25,000, but our overall loss was in excess of £30,000, all because I chased the deal. In other words, I was too eager to do the deal. With hindsight the vendor was controlling the deal, not me, and I always prefer to be in the driving seat.

We paid £53,000 for the land with all the fees and so on and ended up selling it at auction for £28,000. Although we made a loss, we took the view that it was worth losing a little to get the bulk of the money back out so we could use it again.

From this, I learnt that if a deal requires some urgency and has a seven-day completion timescale, there must be a reason. In the majority of cases, it could be a repossession rescue, but even in those scenarios repossessions can be delayed with the right paperwork.

As they say, 'If it looks too good to be true, it probably is'. I learnt a lot from this deal alone that has helped me with lots of land and property acquisitions. My approach to property is simple. If the deal stacks up and works in your favour, do it. If it's proving too much like hard work, don't worry – another one will be along shortly. The investor who chases the deal tends to lose the most money.

You're not always going to get your money back from every property deal. It's the same with refurbishments. You can buy a property and you can do some work and you can have it refinanced, but you may have to leave some money in the deal. It's not the end of the world to leave a bit in; I treat it as if it's enforced savings, like a little piggybank. You'll still have that equity in the property even if you can't access it.

Let me give you an example of what can happen when you chase a deal. When Webuypropertiesfast was trading actively we had a call from a lady who seemed to be in quite a lot of distress and who said that she needed to sell her property fast. She had been through a messy divorce and looked like she had hit the bottle. She told me she had hit rock bottom and now she wanted to get rid of anything that reminded her of all those unhappy years of marriage. The property was a three-bed semi-detached house. It was in good condition so we agreed a deal at £80,000, which was a good buy.

The property was worth around £135,000, and the three estate agents who visited and appraised it each confirmed that this was a realistic ninety-day sale price. The problem was that the £80,000 we needed was tied up in another deal. So we had to try to figure out how we could acquire this property with no money, and yet still make money. Then the seller hit me with a bombshell. It turned out that she wasn't the sole owner; the property was co-owned with her former husband and she wasn't allowed to contact him because of a restraining order. This didn't make things easy, but we were determined not to let the deal slip through our fingers. I offered to act as a mediator between the two of them, but although I had the husband's telephone number I don't like calling people cold, because they don't know who I am or what I'm about. So instead I pushed a note under his door and asked him to call me. In it, I explained that I had been talking to his former wife about buying the property and that he would benefit from the sale proceeds if he could help the transaction along. He seemed pretty pleased by that so we thought everything was going better than we could have hoped.

Then something happened that caused all hell to break loose. Somehow, despite the restraining order, the husband and wife contacted each other and had an almighty falling out, and, even worse, they were refusing to talk to me. In the end I managed to get hold of them both. I had my mobile phone in one hand calling the husband and my landline phone in the other calling the wife. I'd talk to the husband and he'd be effing and blinding and ranting about his side of the story, and then I had to put him on hold and speak to the wife and explain to her what his problems and issues were, without repeating all the effing and blinding, of course. It took about an hour and a half on the phone, with me as a mediator and go-between, but we managed to resolve things to the point where they both agreed that we could sign contracts. I insisted that we did it that evening because I felt that otherwise the deal wasn't going to happen.

Our terms were that once we exchanged, we weren't going to complete for another fifty-six days. They didn't particularly like that because they wanted their money straightaway, as you'd expect, but we needed those fifty-six days because we had a plan for how to make money from this deal without tying up any money. We put the property up for auction, which we could do as we'd exchanged on it and had the consent of the vendors. The guide price was between £90,000 and £95,000 and the terms and conditions specified a completion day for the purchaser that was the same as the day we had agreed with the sellers. It sold at auction for £105,000. The money came into our solicitor's account; the solicitor then paid £80,000 to the vendors and we kept the other £25,000.

Now that wasn't the end of the story. I know the person who bought the property and they allowed the lady to remain there and rent it from them. This was in the days when sale-and-rent-back wasn't a regulated activity. Do you remember I mentioned the lady had a bit of a drink problem? I got a call from our buyer about four weeks after the auction, saying that the lady had burnt the house down. Apparently, she had fallen asleep with a cigarette in her mouth and the whole house went up in flames. Luckily she was okay and, as it turned out, the buyer did alright out of it because the insurance company paid out the whole sum insured and he managed to get the house rebuilt more cheaply. So in a sense everybody involved in this story was a winner.

I learnt from this exercise never to chase a deal. I chased this deal too hard and it caused me far too much grief. I was determined to make it happen no matter what, but I decided afterwards that I really don't want to be one of those people who is chasing around at eight o'clock in the evening trying to get people to sign contracts. If you have to chase around too hard to get a deal done then perhaps it's not a deal you should be doing. Looking back, I could have used my time far better elsewhere and still have made the same amount of money but with a fraction of the grief and hassle.

Typically our advertising for Webuypropertiesfast was generating leads where we'd buy a property for around £80,000 and then re-sell it at a local auction for £95,000, making us about £10,000 after costs. In the great scheme of things this might not seem like a lot of money, but these deals were our bread and butter and we were doing lots of them every month.

By then we had the beginnings of an extensive database of local landlords. I've told you that a lot of what I do started because I needed to solve a problem, and in a sense this is true of our landlord and investor database. It happened like this. Although we were advertising in the local paper for properties to purchase, other landlords and investors were calling us and asking if we had any properties to sell on. Of course, as we regularly attended auctions we were becoming well known in the market. As our database and list of contacts grew we realised we were less dependent on auctions to sell so we modified our strategy.

At that time buy-to-let mortgage providers were actively lending and we realised that by selling our properties to people on our database and putting them in touch with the lenders we could greatly speed up the sales process. I've always liked systems, and this was a great system.

Here's what we did. Let's say our newspaper advert generated a lead and a vendor called us wanting to sell a property worth, for example, £100,000, but we were able to negotiate a price of £70,000. We'd agree the purchase but would then immediately go out to our database and offer the property for, say, £85,000. The market was so warm then that we'd regularly find a buyer on the same day that we agreed to buy it. We'd then exchange on our purchase and our buyer would exchange as soon as possible afterwards, then completion would be simultaneous between all the parties. In other words, we'd buy it and instantly sell it on to our purchaser, who would be able to finance their purchase using the active mortgage lender.

I know that a lot of people got their fingers burnt by being over-exposed to the whole mortgage-lender same-day re-financing system, but at the time it seemed to be one of the greatest things that had ever been available to investors. Here's how it worked:

We'll use the example I've just given of a property that was worth £100,000 but that we could buy for £70,000 and then sell on for £85,000. The buyer would typically arrange a short-term bridging loan of, say, 85 per cent of the purchase price. So 85 per cent of £85,000 would mean they could borrow £72,250. They would have to put £12,750 in to cover the balance. At the same time they'd be able to apply to re-finance through the mortgage lender.

The mortgage lender would lend based on the value and not the purchase price, so they would be able to borrow 85 per cent of £100,000, or £85,000.

What made this system so attractive was that they could draw these funds down immediately upon completion. That meant they could instantly pay back the bridging loan and take out the money they put in to cover the balance.

There were ways and means of doing this where the purchaser didn't even have to physically provide the deposit. Because all of this happened almost simultaneously the bridging was a bit academic, but the upshot of using this process was that the purchaser would be able to buy the property from us with 100 per cent finance.

Many investors throughout the UK were using this system at the time to get 100 per cent finance for their investment properties. We just saw the opportunity to steer our customers in that direction to make it easier for them to buy our properties from us. I love systems, and by systemising and streamlining everything we got to the point where we were routinely doing around thirty deals a month.

'You may be disappointed if you fail, but you are doomed if you don't try.'

Beverly Sills

We Expand the Family Portfolio

Lesson 7: Build a nest egg for a rainy day

Over the years the business has gone in a different direction, but Webuypropertiesfast is still going, although not at the level of those previous halcyon days. Now some say all good things must come to an end, but every cloud has a silver lining.

Inevitably, in 2006 mortgage providers stopped same-day re-financing when the Council of Mortgage Lenders brought in the six-month rule. Principally this was a reaction when things started to unravel after the crash.

The six-month rule essentially says that lenders won't grant a remortgage within six months of a mortgage being advanced or within six months of the borrower buying a property. Some lenders won't grant a new mortgage to a buyer if the seller has owned the property for less than six months. What this meant was that anybody who bought a property from us, and who needed a mortgage to finance the deal, would now have to show their lender that we had owned the property for at least six months before we sold it on. At that time most of our purchasers needed a mortgage so this pretty much killed our flipping business stone dead overnight.

We went from selling around thirty properties a month to selling only five. We were making around £10,000 to £15,000 a time, and I am sure many people wouldn't consider five deals a month to be too shabby, but we were generating far less cash than we had been used to.

We thought about selling through auction again, but that market was slowing down visibly as the recession kicked in. The irony was that with the slowdown in the economy, and in the property market, we still had plenty of leads from people who needed to sell, but the choice of who to sell to was now much more limited. We realised that these leads were far too good to be wasted and after a while the thought struck us that we should be buying the properties for ourselves. This was quite a big change for us because up until then our view had been that we didn't want to be landlords, other than the family portfolio we already held. We would much rather buy and sell, as this generated the same amount of cash as a landlord might receive in rent, over several years, but without all of the responsibilities and hassle of actually being a landlord.

Sometimes, though, you just have to adapt to what's going on around you, and we didn't want to let those deals slip through our fingers. So if we had to be a landlord to make the most of the opportunities we had, so be it. On the plus side, we were buying these properties so cheaply that we were sitting on a considerable amount of equity, which was great.

As with so many other aspects of the business, I became a landlord almost by chance rather than by design. I often think that good things happen to those who try, and here's another example of that. Although same-day re-financing was no longer available, we discovered that if we bought the properties for cash at the lower price, our principal lender would still be happy to re-finance the day after we completed at the higher value.

Although looking back this might seem surprising, we hadn't yet experienced the full force of the credit crunch and we had established a very good relationship with our lender over the years. We had been running a high-volume cash business for a couple of years so I'm sure they felt pretty secure with us and didn't see us as a particularly bad risk. Far from it, they probably saw us as being a very good risk. Whenever we bought a property all we'd have to do was call our lender, talk them through the figures and, shortly afterwards, we'd be able to re-finance and pull out all of our money and use it to buy again.

Some investors got themselves into trouble using the same-day re-financing technique, but I think that's because a lot of them actually pulled out more money than they put in. Sometimes, if you bought a property cheaply enough, you would actually be able to take out more money than you'd put in and could then spend the excess, either on new property investments, which I think was the wisest use of the money, or, as some investors were tempted to do, to live the high life. Even back then I wasn't prepared to do that, and I've made it a rule of mine only to pull out the money I've put in and not take out any extra.

At around that time we cut back heavily on our marketing. Up until then we'd been advertising in almost every publication we could find, looking for properties we could buy to flip on. Now that we were buying for ourselves we needed to tweak the strategy a little.

I'm a firm believer in buying in your local area; I always jokingly say that you need to be able to reach out and touch the properties you own, and most of our current portfolio is within a ten- or fifteen-minute drive of our office. It didn't make any sense to advertise all across the West Midlands anymore; we only needed to advertise locally. Even when we cut back on our advertising we still had more properties to choose from than we could ever possibly buy for ourselves. I guess that was a reflection of the market at the time, which, as we all know, fell very dramatically once the credit crunch fully hit.

As credit conditions began to tighten, it became necessary to be much more aggressive in our negotiating and buying. We weren't sure when, or if, our lender would tighten their lending criteria, so we'd always assume that we would need to put down at least 25 per cent of the purchase price as a deposit. The deposit is only one cost involved in buying property; there are all the other associated costs as well, such as legal fees and mortgage application fees, so the very minimum discount we were prepared to accept from market value was 30 per cent. I imagine this made me somewhat unpopular with the vendors but I couldn't see that there was any way around it.

If we went to see a property and thought it was worth £100,000, our first offer would be £50,000. To many vendors that was probably a very derisory offer,

and nine times out of ten we'd be told to get lost. I think if you're going to be in this business you've got to have thick skin and broad shoulders, especially if you're buying property to let it out as a landlord. As a landlord you know you're going to get called some things and see some things that are going to offend you, so if you're easily offended then being a hands-on property investor might not be the right role for you.

If the initial offer of 50 per cent was rejected, or £50,000 on a £100,000 property, we would then offer £55,000. If the vendor wouldn't bite at that figure we'd just gradually edge up, knowing the whole time that the most we could afford to pay was £70,000. That would give us our 30 per cent discount to cover all the costs. Most of the time we would be able to buy for between £50,000 and £60,000 and rarely had to offer the full £70,000. I should stress that when calculating how much to pay and what discount was required, we would work from our perception of the value and not the vendor's perception. For example, if the property had been on the market for £115,000 but we genuinely thought that the maximum value was £100,000, we would offer 50 per cent of our assessment as the initial offer, and not 50 per cent of their asking price. After all, valuation is subjective and we had no idea how their asking price had been arrived at or who had suggested it. We could only go by what we thought the property was worth after doing some research.

Eventually, and inevitably, our lender began to slow the process down and we were finding it harder to re-finance through them. So we spread our net and went to several high-street lenders who were prepared to lend, although only on standard terms so we'd have to wait six months before we could re-finance. This was frustrating because we were buying very aggressively at the time. After all, if something's worth doing, you may as well go all out for it.

One thing that did help us was that we created our own letting agency in 2008, which provided us with another source of cash flow that we could use as deposits on other properties while we waited out the six months to re-finance the properties we'd bought. It's possible we could have grown the portfolio more quickly if we'd been prepared to be even more aggressive on the financing side as well, but as I've already said, I never liked the idea of taking out more money from a deal than I put in, and that's a principle I've always stuck to.

For example, if I bought a property worth £100,000 for £50,000, in theory I could re-finance at a 75 per cent loan-to-value ratio and pull £75,000 back out. That would give me an extra £25,000 that I could use as a deposit on another property. We never did that, and we never will. We only ever borrowed the £50,000 cash needed to purchase the property in the first place, along with perhaps £2,000 or £3,000 to cover the costs of purchase and financing. Other than that, we would leave the equity in the property. In the long run it increased our cash flow because it meant we weren't paying out so much each month on a higher mortgage, and it left a buffer in the property in case of future price falls or other problems. I feel far more comfortable being geared at 50 per cent than 75 per cent.

A major benefit, though, is that it really does enhance our relationship with the bank. They can see that the portfolio is geared conservatively so they are much more tolerant and helpful when we need to draw down a short-term loan, or when we have a particular situation that requires special terms or is a little bit unusual. It also means that if we ever need access to cash quickly there's plenty of equity within the portfolio overall that we can access without taking ourselves up to ridiculous levels of gearing. In fact, every year, if the profits across the businesses as a whole allow, we'll even make lump-sum payments against our mortgages and reduce the gearing even further.

'Limitations live only in our minds. But if we use our imaginations, our possibilities become limitless.'

Jamie Paolinetti

Double Rent/Triple Income

Lesson 8: Maximise the return from your existing property before purchasing more

There are many avenues / strategies you could apply to increase the revenue from your property, each one has its own advantages. A few options open to you are: Creating a HMO, renting to students or renting to LHA families.

Many new landlords may find these options a great starting point to generate extra income from their properties. This extra income in turn helps to quickly generate the deposit for their next property / project, which can assist them on their way to financial freedom.

Renting to LHA families is an opportunity to increase the rent through a careful and strategic approach, the family in question can be reviewed with the following factors in mind:

- **Mum and Step Dad**
- **Daughter and her child**

Traditionally this would have been a family unit and providing you were content, this would generate the landlord the 3 bedroom rate of the local housing allowance. For example, £120 per week, or £520pcm.

If you were to implement the LHA strategy, you would be able to generate from this family a minimum of £170per week or approximately £735pcm, giving you additional £215pcm in income from this property.

The maximum you could achieve from these tenants using the LHA strategy would be £240per week or just over £1000pcm, which we would all agree is a massive increase from the original rental income.

Now, having read that many investors would be thinking to themselves, how is this possible and more importantly, Is it legal?

I can confirm that everything that has been stated above is completely above board and everything submitted regarding this family is declared to the council by means of the application form. There is no such thing as a 'get rich quick scheme' in property and with that in mind, *never try and pull the wool over the eyes of the local authority.* It will come back to haunt you in the long run. Each local authority around the country will try and analyse the way you have structured the tenancy differently. However, providing you follow the correct guidelines outlined in the government handbook, you should not encounter any issues as this is also the document from which the local authorities source their information.

It is worth noting here, that to apply this strategy you will not have to adapt the property in any way to accommodate this extra income. It is very much paperwork based and is all dependant on how the tenancy is structured. In the property courses I run, I go into great detail about this strategy and ways to structure a tenancy in a positive light.

Now, lets look at tis family make-up in greater detail to see how the new income has been created:

- **Mum and Step Dad**
- **Daughter and her child**

For the purpose of this example, I'm going to assume that the landlord is happy with charging this family £170 per week or £735pcm.

On the basis that the mom and dad are entitled to housing benefit, they are entitled to put in a separate claim although they live in the same property as the daughter and grandchild. Lets work on the basis that the council will offer this couple the shared room rate at £60 per week or £260pcm

The second variable is that the daughter and her child are also entitled to a claim for housing benefit within the same property due to their eligibility. Providing they have filled in the sufficient information and the tenancy agreement is structured correctly, they would be entitled to the 2-bedroom rate of the local housing allowance, which would be approximately (for the purpose of this example) £110 per week or £475.

So £60 + £110 = £170 per week or £735pcm.

Please, please, please, do not then read this and then go off and try and increase all of your tenant's rents without further research on this matter area. This will simply cause you many issues, as I cannot stress the importance of having the correct documentation in place to implement the above strategy.

Providing it has been implemented correctly, this could be considered a win, win situation on all accounts. The landlord wins, as they are now getting a much larger rent for their property without the need to do any additional work. The tenant wins, as all the rent is being covered by housing benefits / local housing allowance. I would like to think that providing the landlord is now in receipt of higher income, they would not pursue the tenant for any top up. As the tenant does not have to pay anything out of their personal purse, you should find that the tenant would remain in the property for a longer period.

Please note that if you are renting to a related family, this cannot be considered as a HMO. You may need to identify the relationship between the tenants, but once proven, this cannot be challenged as a HMO model.

Things to consider:

- How many people are in the property
- Can the property accommodate the number of people
- How many people are eligible and are claiming benefits
- How to structure the tenancy
- How many claim forms are required
- How to apply the information onto the claim form(s)
- The split of the property
- The rental liability per person for the property
- How the new rental income has been achieved
- Could this be considered as contrivance
- How will the council understand this application
- And a few others…

Taking all the above into consideration, providing it is done correctly you can make a lot of extra income by implementing this strategy. Best of all, it costs nothing to implement (unless you wish to come on my LHA Masterclass to learn more…yes, a shameless plug). I run a monthly course that offers a range tailored support dealing with a range of strategies that ultimately deal with increasing your income and educating you further about HMO and LHA strategies.

Should you wish to find out more about maximising your rent from the LHA sector, go to my website where you will be able to find further details about upcoming events. www.arshellahi.com

'There are no traffic jams along the extra mile.'

Roger Staubach

Letting Agents Now?

Lesson 9: Utilise the skill set you already possess to expand your business

I had never intended to be a letting agent, but once again a golden opportunity arose unexpectedly. Here's how it happened.

An investor who had bought quite a lot of properties from the Webuypropertiesfast trading arm of the business contacted me

He said, 'Arsh, I've got a bit of a problem. I have a tenanted property where I asked the council to pay me the rent direct as the landlord, but they decided that there were no reasonable grounds for this, so they've paid the tenant. That tenant got a cheque for eight weeks' rent, and guess what? He's run off. I've just lost a lot of money. That was the best part of £1,000 the tenant has just been given and as far as he's concerned it was Christmas in May. Is there anything you can do to help me, Arsh?'

At that stage I didn't want to divulge all the systems and processes we'd put in place, so I simply offered to look after the property for him, never realising that this was going to evolve: this would be the first of many lucrative deals we would do in lettings.

Of course, as you'll realise by now, I rarely do things the 'normal' way and I wasn't really interested in looking after his property just to receive 10 per cent of his monthly rent, or whatever the standard management fee is. I asked him what rent he wanted and he said £400 per month. I quickly worked out that by using our strategy, the property could let for £550 per month. So I made him this simple proposal. I said to him, 'I'll tell you what. I'll manage the property for you but I won't charge you a fee. Instead, if I can get a higher rent than your £400 a month, I'll keep any excess as my commission.' To be honest, I wasn't sure how he was going to react to that, but he said, 'Arsh, as long as I get £400 a month, I'm happy with that.' We agreed that if I got paid the rent then he would get paid, but I wasn't going to guarantee the rent. We also agreed that I would notify him if any repairs were needed and he would deal with them. At that time I wasn't looking to start a management business, I was just doing somebody a favour and I wanted it all to be as hassle free as possible.

So we found the landlord a tenant and we were really pleased that using our system we let the property for £550 a month. I was making £150 a month for doing very little! That got me thinking and I realised that I was sitting on a potential goldmine. If the landlord had gone to a conventional managing agent who did things the 'normal' way, the property would have been let for £400. From that £400 a month the agent would deduct their 10 per cent commission, or whatever they charged, plus VAT if they had a reasonable size business, so the landlord would only have received, say, £350 per month. On the other hand, the managing agent would only have received £40 per month.

But by doing it my way the landlord got the full £400, we received £150 in commission and everyone was happy! That is almost four times the amount that a conventional managing agent would get for managing an identical property. I realised we could be a very profitable business. Now I hasten to add that my client was extremely happy with what was happening. I'd told him upfront that I would be trying to achieve a higher rent and that I would be pocketing the difference, and he didn't mind that at all. All he wanted was a net £400 and for somebody else to deal with any awkward problems, so he felt as if I was managing his property for free.

In fact, the landlord client was so happy with the service we were providing that, within a relatively short space of time, he transferred his other nine properties to us so that we were managing his whole portfolio.

At that time we still hadn't fully caught on to the fact that we could build a substantial cash flow from this business, so we didn't actively go looking for clients. As things transpired we didn't need to.

Not long after we'd taken on the other nine properties, our client's cousin contacted us. My landlord friend had been telling him about what a great service we provided so his cousin asked if we could we take over his portfolio of thirty properties. Well, of course we could! And we did. As far as they were concerned, they had let their properties for free.

Within a relatively short time period we were taking on client after client, purely through referrals and word of mouth.

By understanding the traditional letting agency model, I adapted it so it is financially more beneficial for both parties. Here's how it works:

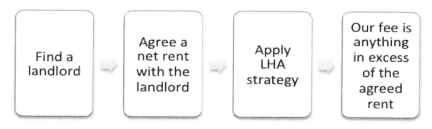

In its simplest form, the letting agency acts as a traditional agency and manages the property on behalf of the landlord client. However, it can be considered very similar to a rent-to-rent strategy, but without guaranteeing the rent. You only need to pay the landlord whilst the property is occupied. All the maintenance can be dealt with by the landlord unless they instruct you otherwise, which can also be quite a lucrative income stream from a business point of view.

You may be wondering what happens if the landlord wants more rent than you think you can get from the tenant. When you are approached by a potential client who is asking for £550 a month, do your research and consider the following:

- What is a the market rate for that area?
- Inspect the house – is it worth it?
- What could you potentially get by implementing the LHA strategy?

If £550 is the maximum you will be able to generate, you must negotiate with the landlord and suggest he takes a lower rent. Here are the pros and cons for him of using you as opposed to a traditional letting agent:

Rent Me Now Service

Pros

Landlord agrees £500pcm –
he will receive £500 with no
other costs charged.
Very few voids on rent
Good service
Occupied quickly
Systemised approach
Landlord is very hands-off
Property suffers more wear
and tear

Cons

May cost more in maintenance

Other Agents 10% Standard Model	
Pros	**Cons**
Agent lets the property for £550. Costs now to consider: 10% management = £55+Vat = £66.00pcm Tenant set up fees – 2 weeks of first month Amount landlord actually gets = £484.00 In the first month of the tenancy, the landlord will only receive circa £240. Not to mention any other costs which agents may charge i.e administration charges etc	Same risks associated with any agent. Expensive maintenance Agents may not be as proactive to find a tenant.

In using this model for the last six years, Rent-me-now has become a thriving agency with a huge income simply by negotiating and dealing with people who may not want the hassle of daily dealings with tenants.

The success of our business is built on three basic principles that we employ when looking for potential tenants.

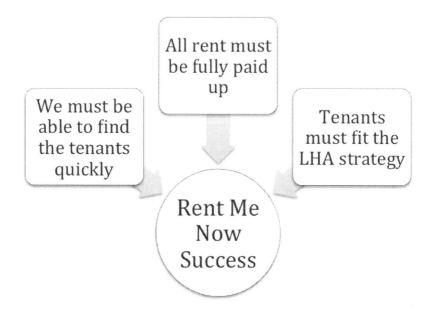

People often ask how we manage to find tenants, and how we manage to find them so quickly. I think they might wonder whether we sacrifice quality for quantity, as it were, but we do have our very own vetting system, which I am sure will come as no surprise.

Here's a quick reminder of how we do this:

1. **Take a reference from a previous landlord**
2. **Check tenant's housing benefit history**
3. **Check their bank statement**
4. **Inspect their current property**
5. **Use your sixth sense**
6. **Have a chat**

Principally there are two ways in which we keep our clients' properties full. I've already said that we gained a lot of business from landlords by word-of-mouth referrals because we do a great job, but we also get a lot of word-of-mouth referrals from tenants, because they equally consider that we do a great job.

My advice is to invest some time in getting to know your tenants. Now I'm not implying going to the pub on a Friday night with them, but just taking the opportunity to be pleasant and treat them with respect. Often tenants who are on benefits are treated poorly by members of the public and can therefore be a little hesitant. This business really is all about building relationships, and I strive to be approachable and offer a listening ear should any of my tenants need someone to talk to.

All this works in our favour when we are looking for new tenants. The world of benefits is a small world, particularly in this area, and friends and families all talk to each other. So when we house a family on benefits and make sure they are okay and that everything is going well, they'll tell their friends and their family. They'll tell them that they have this nice house which is well looked after, that the landlord is good, and that he understands them and their needs. Next thing you know we get a call from their friends or family members asking if we can find a home for them as well. We even offered an incentive scheme for landlords and tenants for any referrals they provided.

The second way we keep our properties full is to use the local newspaper, which has been very successful. One thing that has really helped is making it very clear within the advert that DSS tenants are welcome. Here is an example of the wording of our newspaper ads:

> *Large 3 bedroom house to rent, walking distance to town centre, close to school and amenities, DSS families/housing benefits welcome, low rent/negotiable deposit. Move in today! Call...*

When you are looking for newspapers to advertise in, ensure you place an advert in the local free paper. We often receive more calls from the free newspaper, which is distributed on a Thursday, than we do from our purchased advert on a Wednesday. Gumtree and local groups on Facebook are also excellent places to advertise your vacancies.

Before considering taking on a tenant, there are many factors to consider. These are:

➢ Appearance

➢ Demeanour

➢ Attitude

➢ Punctuality

➢ Organisation

Upon meeting and talking to potential tenants, I always ask them to sit through an informal interview. I ask a number of questions about their previous arrangements. Here are some of the questions I ask:

1. Where are you living at the moment?
2. Why do you want to move?
3. Are you currently claiming housing benefit?
4. Do you have any rent arrears?
5. Are there any disputes with your current landlord?
6. Have you given your landlord notice?
7. How much rent are you paying?

I know the LHA rates for the area, so I can work out from their answer whether they are paying their landlord a top-up. If they are paying a top-up, I'll ask them how they do it. I'll be able to tell from their answer whether they are telling the truth or not and whether the system they describe is realistic or not. After all, I've been collecting top-ups for years now so I know what works and what doesn't. So if it sounds like they're trying it on, they won't go any further in the process. If what they say sounds reasonable, at that stage they are still in the game.

I'll also ask them about their criminal background. There's no point pussyfooting around; if there is anything in their past, we can find out. We can do CRB (now DBS) checks to find out if they have a criminal record, but it's much better if they just come clean about it. If there were offences again children or sexual offences, I wouldn't take them.

I'm also very hard on drugs. Drug dealers are the worst because they know other drug dealers, which means, before you know it, you'll find a little community gathering in your property and you've created a drug den. That's not something you really want to manage or have to deal with. I will take a view on drug takers – that's drug takers who tell me that they're now clean – depending on how long they've been clean and whether we can get some kind of a reference from somebody who has been part of their rehabilitation process.

If the tenant tells me that they've been involved in petty criminal activities like shoplifting or burglary then I'll have to take a view on that. The key question is when did they last commit an offence and, of course, how many offences do they have against their name. If it's just one or two isolated historical incidents, I probably wouldn't hold that against them. If it's an ongoing problem, I don't really want them in my properties.

I might be going off on a bit of a tangent, but here's a story that illustrates just how important it is to vet your tenants and not try to rush the process, because having to deal with drugs can be a nightmare.

I remember having a massive scare when we bought a small commercial unit in the West Midlands. It was only six hundred square feet, which is relatively small, but it is surprising how such a small property can cause such big problems. It was like a small car repair workshop. It had a big roller-shutter door at the front and a small office and toilet block at the back. Because of where it was located we would find that tenants would come in and start a business, and maybe occupy the property for six months, before realising that they couldn't make it work. Then they would disappear and we'd be trying to let the property again and it could be vacant for another six months. Here is what happened when I was approached by a very eager individual who was desperate for the unit, and found myself in bother.

I was approached by someone who was very interested in taking the property, and I signed him up on a six-month tenancy. Because I wanted to get him in quickly I did it all in a hurry and I didn't check his ID thoroughly.

Anyway, he signed the tenancy and took possession and I didn't think about it very much until, towards the end of his six- month tenancy, I had a call from the police to say that he was growing cannabis. Of course I was shocked; finding out that one of your properties is a cannabis farm is bad enough, but I was completely unprepared for what happened next.

The police invited me to go to the station for an interview,

and I assumed I was going there to help them find the tenant or give them as much information about him as I could. When I arrived I was immediately arrested and they started to caution me. They accused me of creating a controlled environment in which to grow cannabis and of colluding with the tenant.

They asked me for all the documents, and I showed them exactly how the tenancy had been prepared and the limited ID that I had taken from the tenant, but at that stage they were not willing to consider that I had nothing to do with it. I was charged and put on bail, and this lasted for seven months. Month after month I had to keep going back because they kept saying that the identification I had taken was insufficient.

Eventually they realised there was no case for me to answer, but it cost me £15,000 in legal fees to defend. I took £5,000 in rent from that tenant over a six-month period but paid out £15,000 in legal bills. That really hurt. Because my various businesses are strong and were cash flowing I was able to sustain that loss, but I don't know what I would have done if I was a first-time landlord. Would a first-time landlord have been able to pay a £15,000 legal bill? It doesn't bear thinking about.

You really have to be careful as a landlord, and you have to be sure you know who you are dealing with and regularly inspect your properties to make sure nothing untoward is happening.

Anyway, back to our interview system. Next, I'll ask them if we can go and have a look at their property, there and then. If they say no, that makes me wonder what they are trying to hide, but if they say yes, we'll jump in the car and go and have a look. Before they walked into the office they wouldn't have dreamt that within half an hour I'd be in their current property, so there's nothing they can conceal from me. If, when I walk in, it's obvious that they don't keep their property in a good condition, then unfortunately there's no way I will sign a tenancy agreement with them. In fairness, sometimes the tenant has done their best to keep the property clean and in good order, but you can see that they've been let down by their landlord, who hasn't maintained the property as they should. If that's the case, and if the vetting is going well, then I will give them a chance. That's how we vet our tenants. It might seem very simple but it is effective.

One Friday afternoon in 2007 I had a telephone call from a man who said, 'I'm going to tell you a little bit about my situation and then you can tell me what you think.' So he told me that he'd been trying to find a property for the last twelve months but he'd struggled and struggled. That instantly began to ring alarm bells for me because you have to wonder, if somebody has been looking for twelve months, why they haven't found anything. It suggests there's a big problem.

So I asked him where he was living at the moment. He said, 'To be completely honest, I'm living in a tent in the middle of a field near Kidderminster.'

Often, when you are dealing with tenants on benefits, you just have to go with your gut feeling, and there's one particular tenant, I think, who proves the point.

Apparently he'd been living in the tent with his niece for twelve months. Although he was on benefits he wasn't able to get any kind of help from anybody, not from private landlords, the local authority, housing associations or anybody.

So he was living in a cold tent in the middle of a field with no electricity and no running water. In my mind I was beginning to picture somebody who was probably quite dirty and old. I know that's a stereotype but, if you were having this telephone conversation, what would you think?

Then he said to me, 'You won't do a credit check, will you? Because if you do that's me as good as done.' I respected his honesty, but out of curiosity I asked him, 'You're in Kidderminster and I'm in Wolverhampton, which is fifteen miles away. How did you get hold of my telephone number?' He said 'It's a funny thing, but the newspaper that you advertise in blew across the field and was stuck to my tent.' By then I was beginning to really warm to him and I began to feel he had something about him. If you can picture the scene, he's in a tent in the middle of a field, and a local newspaper, from Wolverhampton, has somehow blown across to his tent and he's taken the initiative, with all the odds stacked against him, to call me and ask for help. I never do interviews on a Friday afternoon as it's usually pretty frantic in the office, I said to him that he needed to come and see me on Monday morning at nine o'clock. I arrived at the office on Monday morning at eight so I could do a bit of paperwork before opening up, and he was already there waiting outside with his niece. So I took them in for our ten-minute chat and I really liked what I saw.

He and his niece were not at all what I imagined; they were a lot cleaner and a lot more together than I thought they'd be. They brought all their belongings in one carrier bag, along with their tent. The moment I offered them a property he asked, 'Can we use your bin please?' and then they stuck their tent in it!

The point is, you just can't tell unless you take the time to get to know people, which is what I like to think we do with our vetting system. These were perfectly good people who had just fallen upon hard times and couldn't get any help. Because they didn't have any form of security, guarantee or deposit, because they didn't have rent in advance or references, no one would touch them, even though they were homeless. They have been with us for eight years now, their rent is paid up to date and they treat their house like a palace – it's immaculately clean.

That's one of the things I like about being a letting agent and a landlord. I like being able to help people. Unfortunately there's a perception amongst the public that landlords are greedy fat cats, but I think we are in a position to be able to help, and that's what I try to do.

That's partly why our letting agency does so well, because we have a reputation of being a letting agency with a heart. It's true that when we have to be tough we can be, but where we can help, and where it's obvious that somebody is in genuine need, we try to accommodate them.

So on to the last question: how do we make sure that the tenants pay once we've selected them? Again, it's a very simple system. Here's what we do. First, if they live within ten minutes' walking distance of the office, they are expected and required to come to the office to pay their top-up. This is a requirement I make clear from the very start; I guess it goes back to tenants taking personal responsibility. I don't want to drive around 300 tenants' properties to collect top-ups; it's too reminiscent of those Monday mornings driving around like lunatics trying to collect the green cheques. It works much better if they come into the office and bring the top-ups to us. By having tenants come to the office, we can ensure we have regular contact with them, and this system alerts us to any concerns we have about tenants' health, both physical and mental.

If they live slightly further out of town and are more than ten minutes' walk from the office, the second means of paying the rent is for them to pop into a branch of our bank. We give them our account number, and as long as they put their name as a reference on the paying-in slip, we can track how much they've paid and when it came in. This works surprisingly well, and every working day we must have the best part of ten to fifteen or more top-ups paid into our bank account.

Now, I realise there is a certain amount of trust involved in all of this and so it is essential that from the outset the process is set up properly. One thing we are always keen to do is outline to the tenant from day one what their responsibilities are so there are no misunderstandings. And we also outline to them what the consequences will be if they don't pay. Because we know who is meant to be paying and when, we know very quickly if a top-up hasn't come in. If that happens the tenant will get either a telephone call or a text within twenty-four hours asking for either the top-up to be paid or a reasonable explanation given for why not. If they don't respond, either by ringing or texting, then within another twenty-four hours there will be a visit to their front door. If they do ring or text, and they provide a reasonable explanation, we'll accept it, but only on the proviso that they pay double next time, or make an arrangement to catch up as quickly as possible.

In our experience, most pay the balance as soon as they can. After all, as I've already said, most of our tenants are very happy with us. Occasionally we do have problems, even though we're on the case so quickly if payment isn't made, in which case we'll issue them with a notice to quit as soon as possible. We don't do this in a threatening or scary way; we try to be very professional and friendly about it. We'll just point out that our relationship is based on trust and that we trusted them to pay the rent. If they are not able to pay the rent then, unfortunately, under the terms of our agreement, they won't be able to retain the property. They fully understand this, and at this stage many of the hard-core non-payers will have paid up.

If they have genuine difficulties paying, we'll try to work out a payment plan with them. If they are just being difficult and won't pay, we'll pursue our notice to quit and take possession. That's really a last resort because it doesn't benefit us to have an empty property or room with no rent coming in. We work with the tenant, and by helping them we can cut the number of voids. We've arranged things so that we don't have to physically go and collect the top-up, but if you have to I suggest you collect it on the same day that the tenant receives their benefits.

I was talking to a landlord the other day and asked him how he collects his top-ups. He told me it was an absolute nightmare because he goes out once a week to collect them from all of his tenants. The problem is that his tenants aren't all paid their benefits on the same day. So, for example, if a tenant is due to pay a top-up on a Monday, I would be insistent that they pay it on a Monday because you can be almost sure it will be spent by Tuesday,

Wednesday, Thursday and certainly by Friday. Therefore, you need to arrange your collections to coincide with when the tenants actually have the money in their hands.

'I am a great believer in luck, and I find the harder I work, the more I have of it.'

Thomas Jefferson

Rent-to-Rent Landlords Next!

Lesson 10: You can make more money by simply controlling someone else's assets

Over the last few years, rent-to-rent has become one of the most popular property strategies to implement. With its ease and 'low-cost' entry to the market, it seems everyone is out to try to get on the rent-to-rent ladder.

In 2013 I challenged myself to see if I could really make this work for me. I was completely new to the strategy and pretty much learnt all that I needed to know from social media forums, reading up on all the legislation behind the strategy, and I did what I do best – I went out and took all of the opportunities that came my way.

Perhaps it's worth noting that I started this strategy from scratch with no knowledge. Within twelve months this has become a cash-flow generator, which brings in more than £10,000 every month. If I can do it, so can you.

This all started when I was approached by someone who had had enough of being a landlord, and who wanted to hand his keys back to his mortgage company. He'd been with another letting agency for quite a few years and allegedly they had run off with £10,000 of rent. Now that seems like quite a lot of money because an average single-let property in Wolverhampton generates between £5,000 and £6,000 in rent a year, which would have meant the landlord didn't receive his rent for two years. Anyway, he walked into the office one day and he just handed me the keys and asked me to buy the property from him. Well, you know by now that I always like to say yes, and so I said, 'Let's talk about it.' He said he wanted £57,000 for the property, and he said, 'If you don't buy the property from me, I'm just going to hand the keys back to the mortgage company.' At this point, the market value for the property was approximately £60,000 with an outstanding mortgage of £54,000.

Because of the amount he owed the mortgage company, I couldn't purchase the property from him, but I presented him with an alternative offer.

I said to him, 'Why don't I rent the property off you and then I'll multi-let it?' He didn't seem very impressed by this, and replied that his worry was that he would end up chasing me for the rent. So I persuaded him that wouldn't be the case and I offered to guarantee the rent as long as he'd agree to allow me to multi-let.

He told me that his monthly mortgage payment was £450, so I offered to give him a guaranteed rent of £275 a month. You're probably wondering why he would rent it out to me for £275 a month if his mortgage was £450 a month. My thinking behind this was that he hadn't seen any rent on his property for the last two years, which meant he had paid his mortgage company £450 every month from his own pocket. So instead of having to pay £450 a month I was giving him the opportunity to only pay £175 a month. On top of that, as his outstanding mortgage was £54,000, he had at least £3,000 of equity in the property, but, over the next ten years, hopefully that would increase as the market recovered. So by helping him service his loan, he would benefit from future capital growth. In ten years' time his equity may have grown from £3,000 to £40,000 or even £50,000.

We agreed the deal and we now multi-let the property using our LHA strategy and receive £650 a month for it. So we are making £375 a month on this property that we don't own, and in which we have no finance tied up.

Here are some of the other benefits of using this strategy to acquire property:

1. No 25 per cent deposit required
2. No mortgage required
3. No solicitor required
4. No surveyor required
5. YOU determine the terms of negotiation

This transaction happened pretty much by chance. I had no idea he was going to walk into my office that morning, or what he wanted to talk about when he first sat at my desk in front of me. I could see that I could make this strategy work, and so since May 2013, at the time of writing we have done fourteen deals similar to this. We've started to advertise for landlords because we want more of this type of property. This is a great cash-flow strategy. As purists, some investors might wonder why I'd want to take on a property without buying it. The great thing about these deals is that you can control the property and the cash flow without having to take out finance and put down a 25 per cent deposit. You haven't got the same level of legal fees, you haven't got to pay a survey fee, and you haven't got to deal with a mortgage company.

My theory to this strategy is: if we buy a property using finance, we are then committed to pay the bank their monthly mortgage for its whole term. The beauty of agreements like this is that we always include a term allowing us to give a month's notice and walk away at any point, but if the landlord wants to take the property away from us, for whatever reason, he has to buy us out at a price reflecting the unexpired period of our contract. We also make sure that the rent we agree is fixed for the whole seven-year period.

Most of the deals we have done have been for single lets, but we've just taken on an HMO. The landlord was using other letting agents, but they couldn't keep all the rooms occupied. It is a six-bed HMO but it usually only had three or four rooms occupied at any one time.

The property consists of:

£325pcm	• Each of the five bedsits makes
£430pcm	• 1 x studio flat
£2,055pcm	• The property generates
£1,100pcm	• We pay the landlord
£500pcm	• Utility costs
£545pcm	• Cashflow
£6,540 per annum	• Equivalent to

Over the next seven years, it will generate £45,780 for us.

Remember, this is all without buying it, without having to pay anything up front, and all I do is keep all of that money to one side and use it to pay off the mortgages in our portfolio.

Obviously we're not against buying a decent property if the deal makes sense, but if you think about it, a landlord can come into my office today, give us the keys and we can do a deal there and then and start renting it out straightaway.

It probably sounds a bit stereotypical, talking about tired and weary landlords. Not every deal we've done has been with a tired landlord. One property is actually owned by a practice, a group of professionals. These are really busy people who didn't want to rent a property out and manage it for themselves, which is why they engaged the services of a managing agent. The problem was that the managing agent was constantly interrupting them during working hours, saying you need to do this or you need to do that. The other problem was that, as so often happens, the agent was having trouble keeping the property fully occupied. So in the end they got very frustrated by the whole situation.

They approached us and offered to sell us the property, which comprised five units: three single studios and two one-bedroom flats. They said we could buy it for £175,000. At that time we didn't even think the property was worth £125,000, never mind £175.000, and so we said, 'Sorry it's not for us, we wish you the best of luck and hope it all goes well.' We could see that they really wanted to do some kind of a deal, so we offered them £80,000, which they were never going to accept, but we parted on good terms and I didn't hear anything from them for a few months.

A few months later they came back to us and said they still hadn't sold it, the property was still only half occupied and they needed some ideas as to what they could do. They actually made the suggestion that we rent the property from them, and they offered it to us at £97 a week for each flat. Well, we couldn't make that work because all we would be doing was working to pay the landlord and not make any money so, again, we had to say no thanks and wish them the best of luck. Again we parted on good terms, but they came back a little more quickly this time and asked us what we could offer. We offered £50 a week per room, which we thought was a good offer, but they laughed at that and said, 'Okay, lets meet halfway at £75 a week per room.'

Again we explained that it had to work on our terms because we'd be taking on all the risk. Eventually, we agreed a deal at £52 a week per room; we only went up £2 and they came down £23, which felt pretty good. We rent out each of the flats for £105 a week, meaning that we make £53 a week on each flat, which is £265 a week in total. And what have I done for that? I haven't had to do anything.

The property is already set up and was refurbished, with each room having its own central heating system with brand new boilers and five-year warranties. The group of professionals still pay the insurance, and our agreement is very simple. Anything to do with the structure of the property is their responsibility; anything internally is our responsibility.

The advantage we have is that we find it easy to keep all of these properties occupied and let. It's easy for us just to bolt this onto our existing system. That property is generating £265 a week, which is £13,780 a year in pure profit, and we haven't had to do anything for it. A standard buy-to-let investor would have to have two single lets, without mortgages, to make that kind of money, and even if we bought cheap properties we'd have to spend at least £100,000 on a property to generate an income like that. It costs me nothing to do a deal like this, and there are so many more out there waiting to be done.

We are constantly looking to increase the number of our properties, and we are advertising very aggressively and touting for landlords. We've got advertisements in local papers all around our patch. We see it as being a very easy way to pay down the mortgages on all our other properties.

If you are considering rent-to-rent, here are some of the basic principles:

In rent-to-rent, you find a property that a landlord is looking to rent out, you offer to rent it from them and then sublet it. In order to make it viable, it is common practice to rent the property out by the room (multi-let the property).

A simple step by step process:

> **Step 1.** You rent a property on a single-let basis from a landlord
> **Step 2.** You get permission to rent out rooms individually
> **Step 3.** You rent out the property by the room (turning a single let into four to six separate lets)
> **Step 4.** You receive multiple rents, pay your single-let rent and utility bills, and bank the difference

Providing you follow these basic principles, you should be able to generate a lot more than you are paying the landlord, therefore creating cash flow from the property.

Please be aware that before you embark on this journey you check out whether you are in an 'Article 4' area. Article 4 directions are made when the character of an area of acknowledged importance would be threatened. They are most common in conservation areas. If you are unaware of the Article 4 directive, I believe the RLA website (www.rla.org.uk) has an updated list of Article 4 areas, of which there are currently around thirty.

As you would need to create a HMO, you also need to be aware of the relevant legislation. This includes:

- Article 4 – where applicable
- HMO licensing – two-storey or three-storey?
- Selective licence – where applicable

Why I decided to utilise this strategy:

Believe it or not, rent-to-rent is not a new strategy. It has been around for a long time but has only become popular since the tightening up of the mortgage market. Being able to acquire a property with no or very little money has made it very popular with property investors, as it's something both 'beginners' and more seasoned investors like me can implement.

The core reason I decided to utilise this strategy was purely that it allowed me to grow an additional business income stream within a very short timeframe by using my business skill set.

Every property investor should have a short-, medium- and long-term strategy. For me these are defined as:

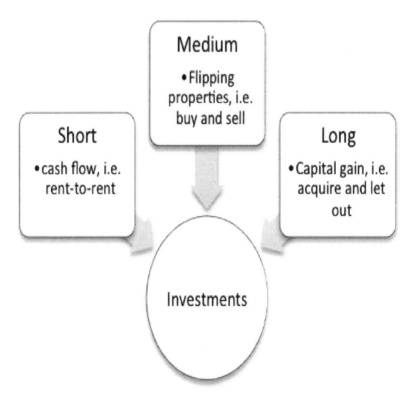

A few deals I have done recently that have cost me nothing to acquire are:

Example No 1 – Crowther Street, Wolverhampton

I came across this property via another investor who couldn't make it work as a rent-to-rent. The property admittedly isn't in the best of areas and will only attract a certain clientele, that is, LHA tenants.

The previous investor was paying the landlord £450pcm and trying to let each room out at £300pcm. In theory this property should have made money, but the problem they found was that they couldn't let the rooms out as they struggled with the area.

After handing the property back to the landlord, they kindly gave me their contact details to see if I could assist.

I visited the property and saw that it had already been turned into an HMO. I negotiated a new rent with the landlord at £350pcm on a seven-year lease and now I have each room let at £75 per week, or £325pcm, with total rental income of £1,300pcm.

Let's have a look at how this works financially:

Rent achieved:	£1,300 pcm
Landlord's rent:	£350 pcm
Utilities:	£350 pcm
Profit from property:	£600 pcm
Money spent on property:	£0
Money used to acquire property:	£0
Amount property will generate over 7 years:	£50,400

Example No 2 – Park Crescent, Wolverhampton

Now this property is rather strange, as this was a property I was hoping to buy myself. I saw it for sale and approached the agent. I was told it was sold subject to contract and the purchaser was looking to turn it into an HMO.

I kept an eye on this property as I watched the successful purchaser create an HMO. I also went to visit him to see what his intentions were, and he told me he would fully manage the HMO himself

The project took approximately eight months in between the landlord's other commitments, and in all fairness he did the work to a very good standard. The property was converted into a ten-bed HMO with communal lounge, three bathrooms and a separate toilet, over three floors. It included leather sofas in the main lounge and flat-screen TVs, and was clearly aimed at the professional market – something I had very little experience of.

The landlord said he would keep me in mind as I put together a proposal I thought both parties would benefit from. I wanted this property as it would need very little maintenance as everything was brand new. Admittedly I was a little worried that benefits tenants would wreck it so I had to adapt to a new market to make it work.

I have to admit that my competitive nature also wanted this property as the landlord instructed another letting agent to help with finding tenants. But having got the job, the other agent was quickly de-instructed. The smallest things in life make me happy.

The landlord had five viewings over two weeks, and then he decided to call me to take me up on my offer. I asked why he only lasted two weeks. His response: 'I'm a mortgage broker. I'm too busy to meet with tenants who fail to turn up.' Within two weeks, I had fully let the property with 'professionals', which was a completely new market to me, and I had to learn new systems to accommodate it. So far, it's working well.

Here's how it worked financially:

Rent achieved:	£3,750pcm
(9 rooms at £85 per week & 1 at £100 per week)	£865 per week
Landlord's rent:	£1,200pcm
Utilities:	£500pcm
Profit from property:	£2,050pcm
Money spent on property:	£0
Money used to acquire property	£0
Amount property will generate over 7 years:	£172,200

Example No 3 – Former care home, Coseley, Wolverhampton

I was approached by the owner of a care home that had been shut for four years as it no longer complied with the necessary regulations. I visited the property and found it was ideal for an HMO.

It was a nineteen-bed residential care home that was almost brand new. It had all the fire doors, fire alarms and furniture in place, and it was in a great location.

Originally the vendor wanted to sell the property, however, he was somewhat in denial about its value. He was after £700,000, which was based on its value as a care home, which it clearly was not. I offered £300,000 but he declared that he could not afford to sell at that price as his mortgage was more.

After some negotiation, he agreed to let the property to me on a long-term basis. I agreed a seven-year lease at £1,500pcm.

The property is now fully let out and it is going to be a great cash-flow generator. However, for me, this wasn't the key reason I wanted this property. I also wanted to help the vendor try to sell it. As the building sits on quite a substantial plot of land, we have agreed legally that should I get planning permission to develop it, I will get 50 per cent of the uplift in sale value above £300,000.

For example, if the development plot sells for £500,000, I would have to give the owner £400,000, but I would keep £100,000 (half of the uplift in value) plus the seven years' rental income.

Let's have a look at how this works financially:

Rent achieved:	£7,000pcm
(19 rooms at £85 per week):	£1,615 p/w
Landlord's rent:	£1,500pcm
Utilities:	£1,000pcm
Profit from property:	£4,500pcm
Money spent on property:	£0
Money used to acquire property:	£0
Amount property will generate over 7 years:	£378,000
Plus 50% lift if property sells for £600,000:	£150,000
Income made from property over 7 years:	£528,000
Cash flow from these three properties pcm	£7,150
Cash flow per year:	£85,800

'Never look down on someone – unless you are helping them up.'

Jesse Jackson

HMO Owners too...

Lesson 11: Don't listen to people who tell you it won't work

We own quite a few HMOs, but two of my favourites were never intended to be HMOs. Here's how we ended up with one of the largest HMOs in the West Midlands, one that everybody told us wouldn't work. When we first came across this property in 2006, it wasn't actually an HMO, it was a seventeen-bedroom care home in West Bromwich, just off the high street. I have always been an advocate for care homes as they are set out in a similar fashion to an HMO; therefore whenever I see a care home for sale, I endeavour to acquire it. The building was let on a ten-year lease to a care home operator who had already been in occupation for a year, so they had nine years remaining on the lease. They were paying £60,000 a year and there was a personal guarantor for the rent on the lease. On the face of it this was a very attractive deal because it was on a full repairing and insuring lease, which means that the tenant was responsible for undertaking all of the repairs as well as insuring the premises, which meant that we would be receiving the £60,000 net after all costs.

We paid £480,000 for it, so with an income of £60,000 per annum the property was yielding 13.5 per cent. At that time the market was good and we were aware that the valuers were putting values on secondary investment properties like this at the equivalent of ten times the rental income. On the basis that we had what we thought was a strong covenant occupying the property for another nine years, we thought it should be saleable at around £650,000. We put it in a local auction with a guide price of £550,000, hoping to get around £600,000 and make a quick £120,000 profit. It was a great plan but there was one fatal flaw: it didn't sell. We tried a couple of other auctions, and it still didn't sell. Obviously we were disappointed, but it was giving a good yield and decent cash flow so we decided we'd just keep it. The property sat well within the remit of our requirements:

a) Could create an uplift
b) Could be sold for a profit
c) If a and b fail, we could retain it to generate a decent income

Everything was fine until a year later when the care home operator defaulted and the company running it became insolvent. I had no option but to start chasing the guarantor, who then declared themselves bankrupt, which left us in a bit of a pickle. Financially it left us with a drama because we weren't sure that we could keep up the mortgage payments. Practically it left us in an awkward position because the property was in West Bromwich and we were based in Wolverhampton, which is about thirteen miles away. It really looked as if we'd bitten off more than we could chew and this one property was going to ruin us.

We had to put our thinking caps on and come up with something quickly.

Our first thought was to approach local housing associations, charities and the local authorities to see if they would rent this property from us, but each and every one of them said that the property was way out of scale for their requirements.

By that time we had a few HMOs and we knew how to manage them, but nothing as large as a seventeen-bedroom property. We have a number of four-, five-, six-, seven- and eight-bedroom

HMOs, but not seventeen people all in one house. As a last resort and, being totally frank, out of desperation, we considered letting the individual rooms as bedsits and running it as an HMO. We seriously doubted whether we'd be able to manage an HMO of this size, and it scared the living daylights out of us. But because there were no other obvious occupiers for it, we didn't think we had any alternative but to turn it into an HMO despite our reservations. Sometimes though, as they say, needs must. After all, we still had outgoings to cover, such as the mortgage repayments and the council tax, even though the property was vacant.

Here's a crazy thing. Although the property was already too big for most purposes, the accommodation wasn't used very efficiently. There was a large area on the ground floor to the rear of the property that was like an entrance hall, but we thought it was a complete waste of space. So rather than sticking to a seventeen-bedroom HMO we applied for planning permission and building regulations to change the internal accommodation and actually increased it to twenty-three bedrooms. We didn't have to change the footprint of the property, we merely made use of the excess space. I shared my vision with a local architect who felt I was over-developing it. I could see that this architect didn't know enough about HMOs, and I contacted an old serving architect who we used for our development projects. After careful consideration, he was able validate my argument for increasing the density to a twenty-three-bed HMO. We submitted the application and within two months it was approved.

We were well aware of the scale of the task at hand. It was a major project because all the letting rooms had to be wired and metered individually before being connected back to the main fuse board, and we had to make sure the electricity provider could connect us with a proper three-phase electrical supply. That alone cost more than £23,000.

I'm nothing if not stubborn, and if somebody doubts I can do something, I do my best to try to prove them wrong. So we ended up with a twenty-three-bedroom HMO, which, to this day, is always more than 90 per cent occupied and generates £120,000 a year in rent. What looked like being a complete disaster that could have destroyed us financially is now one of our best cash-flowing properties. In February 2015, the building was valued at a staggering £1.2 million. The property is included in the ultimate HMO tour on my monthly course. Attendees can view the floor plans, and a guided tour outlines how it was converted.

HMOs do not have to be huge. One of our smallest was never intended to be one, but we saw an opportunity in doing so. When we bought this property it was a two-bedroom terraced house, and our initial idea was to sub-divide it and split the ground floor and the first floor into two separate flats. However, we had a bit of trouble with the next-door neighbours, who were not keen on our plan. They said they would lodge a formal objection if we applied for planning consent. We initially assumed they would try to block an application, and the consensus was it would be refused. So instead of converting it to two flats we decided to create a four-bed HMO. Under planning legislation in the UK, providing we were not in an Article 4 area, we would not require planning permission for anything up to a 6-bed HMO. Therefore we were well within our rights to do so. The neighbour who initially opposed two tenants would now have four.

In practice, each letting room is self-contained with its own kitchen area and en-suite shower room, and although this property started life as a two-bedroom terrace, the accommodation works well and each room has plenty of space. This is despite the fact that when our architect first saw it he said it would never work as an HMO and we had to persuade him otherwise. I don't think we've ever had a vacancy in that property – it's been at 100 per cent occupancy the whole time we've owned it. We initially paid £40,000 for it and had to spend £20,000 on the refurbishment. On the basis that we had to spend £60,000 to purchase and refurbish it, the property now generates rental income of £20,000 per annum and has created a 33 per cent return on investment. Since starting this project in 2010, the property would have already paid for itself, and according to a commercial valuation by Lloyds, it has been valued at £200,000 based on ten times it annual rent.

This is one of the reasons I love buying and holding HMOs – the returns can be phenomenal, especially if you know how to structure them. We currently have one house that has been stripped back to the bare brick and is being converted by our builders, and we are also in the process of acquiring a nineteen-bedroom care home and are waiting to exchange contracts. You may think I'm a glutton for punishment after the story of the other care home, but once we acquire this we will put in for planning consent to increase its capacity to twenty-three or twenty-five beds.

The bare-brick property is a four-bed semi-detached house, which will be a seven-bed HMO when it's finished. We bought it for £108,000 and will spend about £50,000 on the refurbishment, so in total it is going to cost about £160,000 including legal fees. Once it's let it will generate around £35,000 a year, which is a return of almost 22 per cent. Even on a net basis, after paying the mortgage and other costs, it's going to be yielding around 17 per cent per annum and, valued on an investment basis as an HMO, it will be worth £300,000 to £550,000, so we will have increased the capital value by £140,000 based on a value of £300,000.

That's what I love about HMOs. You can buy an ordinary house that will be valued on the basis of what we could call its 'bricks-and-mortar' value, in other words as a single-family residence, but by obtaining the proper planning consent, building regulation consent and, where necessary, a licence for use as an HMO, the property can be valued on a commercial basis as a going concern. This is great if you obtain finance because if you approach the right lender the valuation will be based on the investment value and not the bricks-and-mortar value.

The investment value reflects the income-earning potential of the property and values the cash-flow. I will discuss the definitions in greater detail later in the book. I won't go into the technicalities of how valuations like this are done, but in simple terms they multiply the income by a figure to get to the end value. In our area the standard basis of valuation is to multiply the rent by seven. This multiplier will vary across the country, but seven seems to be our local rate. This means valuers currently consider an appropriate return for this type of property to be 14.28 per cent.

Not all lenders will lend on the basis of the investment value; some will still stick with the bricks-and-mortar valuation. If you can find a lender who will lend on investment value, and if you buy the right property, it's more than possible to pull all of your money back out again after the completion of the works, which means that it's possible to build a substantial portfolio of HMO properties. You can buy a property, re-finance it, get your money back out, and then go and buy another one.

You may be asking yourself what's all the hype about HMOs. It's very simple: *cash flow.*

Investors are drawn to this strategy because of the high level of cash flow an HMO can produce, and the low risk of a property being completely vacant. Here is a beginner's guide to establishing your very own HMO.

Below is a step-by-step process of how to assess the potential of an HMO:

First stage – Looking for the property

Some say this is the most difficult part of the whole process. Having heard hundreds of speakers around the country talking about HMOs, the first thing they say is that HMOs must be close to town centres, on the main bus routes and close to local amenities. I agree with all of the above, however, the first thing you must do in your attempt to acquire a property is be clear of the market you are aiming for.

For instance, are you hoping to explore the student market? If so, the secondary implication you need to bear in mind is location: are you near a university? If you are aiming to cater for young professionals, you want to be close to the city centre. Is it the LHA market? Do you need to be close to the local off-licence? (Just kidding!) The location of the property will also have an impact on the price of the HMO. A property closer to the city will cost near enough double one on the outskirts.

Only once you have understood what you are aiming to achieve can you consider the location. As I cater for the LHA market, location is not the key factor for me as an experienced landlord. I have purchased properties on the outskirts of the city, and my own business partner questioned whether this was a challenge too far; however, this is the HMO that has never had an empty room from the day it was created.

These are some of things you should be looking at before you start your journey in the HMO segment of the property market. I hate to say it, but there are far too many people selling the 'HMO dream', boasting that they make £1,000 or more per month in cash flow from their property, but I regret to inform you that very few HMOs generate this level of cash flow, and we'll look at the figures in greater detail later.

Stage 2 – Found The Property

Once you've found the property, the next question is how are you going to make it work. Undoubtedly property can be a very lonely path at times, especially when you have just purchased it. You have to ask yourself an array of questions, including:

- How any rooms can I get in here?
- Do I let it as all bills inclusive or exclusive?
- Furnished or unfurnished?
- Self-manage or letting agent?
- What happens if someone doesn't pay?

The most important question for me is what can I do with this property should all else fail. Will it work as a single let? Can it work as a single let? Calculating your risk is an essential part of being an efficient landlord or property investor.

When I view a property, I look at it from a flow point of view. How does it flow? When you come in off the street are you walking directly into a room or a hallway? I look at the room sizes and, more importantly, where the kitchen and bathrooms are situated.

The ability to add value to a property is essential as this is a means of generating cash flow and expanding your business. No one wants to buy a property, maintain it, put in blood sweat and tears and then find it's worthless.

The type of property I generally go for is three- or four-bed semi-detached houses that are not in the city centre but are easily accessible via public transport. The reason for this is simple. The cost of the property is less and yet occupants can still enjoy 'city living' by being able to get there with ease. I also look for properties where the local amenities are close by, such as shops and supermarkets.

It is fair to say that I am not your average HMO investor, purely because I don't believe in letting people live in the property and not be in complete control of the utility bills. I have seen landlords across the UK complain about how tenants abuse the heating by leaving it on continuously. Tenants are less likely to heat your HMO as though it were a tropical island if they have to foot the bill themselves. Yes, there are methods to try to control that by putting fair usage clauses into tenancy agreements, but whether they decide to pay up or not is another question.

Utility Costs / Financials

In my opinion, a HMO that offers all-inclusive rent does not actually make much money. Let's look at how I see it:

Standard HMO

Five-bed HMO where all bills are included:

Rent per room:	£300pcm inclusive
5 rooms:	£1,500pcm
Minus costs	
Mortgage:	£400pcm on average
Utilities:	£400pcm
Total cash flow after costs:	£700pcm

But we haven't considered other costs.

Void period at 20% (equivalent to one room being vacant):	£300pcm
Letting fees at 15% on 4 rooms:	£180pcm
Maintenance:	£50pcm
Total profit:	£170pcm

Now ask yourself, has it been worth it? If you have two rooms empty in a month, your HMO has just lost money! More importantly, you could have generated more cash flow from the property as a single let.

My HMO

Five-bed HMO where all bills are paid by tenants:

Rent per room:	£430pcm exclusive
5 rooms:	£2,150pcm
Minus costs	
Mortgage:	£400pcm on average
Utilities:	£0pcm (all tenants are responsible for their own bills)
Total cash flow after costs:	£1,750pcm

But we haven't considered other costs.

Void period at 20% (equivalent to one room being vacant:	£430pcm
Letting fees at 15% on 4 rooms:	£250pcm approx.
Maintenance:	£50pcm
Total profit:	£1,020pcm

I set my HMOs up correctly from day one. I tend to spend a bit more at the outset, but I believe that once I have an HMO set up correctly, I shouldn't have to worry about it for at least ten years. Of course I will have a few maintenance issues, but as everything is brand new I won't have issues with damp and so on.

Each room is metered but is supplied by the energy supplier as opposed to me selling them the tokens. It is worth noting that my HMOs are very self-sufficient. I do not want to be the landlord that gets called at eight o'clock of an evening to go and sell the tenant a token.

Having said that, you must also consider the price point of your property and the market you are housing. Ask yourself: how does your property compare to others in the area? If you are charging £300pcm exclusive and other landlords are charging £300pcm inclusive, who will these people prefer to live with? Are you going to be left with long voids? You can only answer this once you have carried out your market research and due diligence, which I hope you would have done prior to purchasing the property.

En-suites or Off-suites

When looking at a property, the first thing to look at in a room is whether you can fit in an en-suite. If so, where? I like to give every room their own en-suite, which means that the property has to be adapted for the additional plumbing and drainage.

As a student one of my worst experiences was the communal bathroom, which was not maintained to a decent standard. It would take me ten minutes to clean it before I used it. Therefore I decided on my property journey that residents in my HMOs would have their own bathrooms. As a result, I have found that tenants seem happier as they cannot complain about somebody else's mess.

If there is already a bathroom close to one of the rooms, I usually give the occupant of that room sole use of the bathroom – calling it an 'off-suite' – and put en-suites in the other rooms. The person with the off-suite has the same amenities as everyone else, if not bigger and better, and you have still utilised the space within the property and saved money on the renovation. However, if the family bathroom is large enough, maybe you should consider turning it into a room to generate more income from the property.

Communal Space

As ruthless as it sounds, the next thing I look at is the communal living space within the property to see if it can be turned into additional rooms. Again something of a rare breed, I do not offer my tenants any form of communal space. It may seem strange to do this, but I believe that if you have five or six unrelated people who are completely unknown to each other, it is only a matter of time before they have a disagreement. In order to minimise arguments and conflict between tenants, I create their living space in their room, where they must, eat sleep and live, almost like a mini studio, but all within planning and building regulations and housing standards guidelines.

Kitchen

As we are all aware, every property has a kitchen, or at least should have. I simply leave this in and potentially allocate it to a tenant, as with the bathroom. In each room, I give the tenant a tea-making facility, which is perfectly acceptable by UK national guidelines. Should a planning officer come round and ask if I have created self-contained units, I am confident in saying that there is still a communal kitchen on site that is available for every tenant to use should they wish. The reality is that the person we allocate the kitchen to is the only person that uses it.

Each room has a sink unit and worktop along with a wall unit for the tenants to store their food. What tends to happen is that the tenant purchases a microwave and uses that space to cook in.

I would advise all landlords to make sure that there is fire safety equipment on site to cater for this. Something as simple as a fire blanket would assist should anything happen. After all, prevention is better than cure.

'Winners are not those who never fail, but those who never quit.'

Edwin Louis Cole

Funding HMOs

Lesson 12: Know your numbers – if all else fails, know how and where to exit.

One of the questions I am most frequently asked is how I fund my HMO projects and whether I manage to get all my money out of the deal.

Types of Funding Available

In the short term, if you are looking to re-finance your property once it is converted into an HMO, I would suggest using the following few options to purchase the property initially:

Cash
Bridging finance
Joint Venture funding

Not everyone will have cash readily available, but the other two options are well within everyone's grasp.

Although I appreciate that bridging finance is expensive, I always ask myself: would I prefer to do the deal than not do the deal? If the answer is yes, I would use bridging funding. It has helped me fund deals where other banks would have turned away the property. More importantly, if the transaction is time sensitive, bridging finance can be arranged and drawn down in a matter of days. A bank could take weeks or even months to arrange and all be subject to valuation. Many still ask whether it is right to value an HMO on its bricks-and-mortar value or on its investment value. I always look at every deal from two points of view:

- What would I like to achieve from the property?
- How would the bank see this investment from a risk point of view?

Undoubtedly it has become increasingly difficult to finance properties that have been converted into HMOs. As a result, banks have tried to put subtle barriers in place to prevent every investor from doing so.

Some of the areas lenders ask about are:

- Experience of the investor (first-time investor?)
- Existing HMO owner
- Portfolio size
- Income details (is it all from property?)

Prior to 2006, lenders were happy to re-finance a property according to its market value, allowing the investor to pull out all their money (providing they purchased the property below market value). Now, they want the property investor to have some 'money left in the deal', or, as they consider it, 'hurt money'.

In other words if the investor got into difficultly and the property was repossessed, the bank would have some comfort knowing that the investor was also feeling some personal financial hardship.

Bricks-and-Mortar vs Investment Value

My personal belief is that HMOs should be valued as a commercial entity, as they are in their own right a commercial product. I don't agree with mortgage lenders who attempt to value any HMO on a bricks-and-mortar basis.

Definitions of The Types Of Valuations

Bricks-and-Mortar Value – Where a property is valued in comparison with its neighbouring properties. For example, if the neighbouring properties are valued at £100,000, on a bricks-and-mortar valuation, providing the property is similar, it should not be too far off this figure. Estate agents generally use this method.

Investment Value – A property is generally valued on its investment value or a multiplier of its income when it is being run as a business or being sold as a going concern. A typical example would be a shop that is being sold as a running business.

For the HMOs I have created, I could argue that they can no longer be classified as a family or residential dwelling. For example, in all of them each room has its own en-suite, along with a thirty-minute fire precaution door, door closer, thumb-turn lock and grade-one fire alarm. I'm pretty certain that any family dwelling next to an HMO on a residential street would not have this kind of equipment. This is because the HMO has been set up to house five or six individuals and all the necessary precautions have been taken to deal with any eventuality.

I use the analogy that it is almost like trying to value a hospital in comparison to a supermarket. The two are not comparable, and so should not be classified in the same way. Furthermore, an HMO will generate far more rental income than a standard single-let property. So as the HMO has been set up as a commercial property, it should benefit from being valued on a commercial investment basis.

However, for many regular HMO investors who operate on an 'all bills included' model, it could be argued that as they have not done enough of a refurbishment on the property and may have merely put fire doors on, their HMOs should be valued on a bricks-and-mortar basis.

When valuing a property, the surveyor must also comment on whether the bank would be able to sell it as a single dwelling should it need to repossess it or take back control.

If a standard HMO still only has one bathroom and one kitchen and the investor has simply put locks on the doors, I would agree with a bricks-and-mortar valuation as it would be very easy to convert it back into a single dwelling.

Lenders

There are only a few lenders in the HMO market. These are:

- Lloyds
- Aldermore
- Shawbrook
- The Mortgage Works
- Paragon
- Keystone
- And one or two others

From my experience, getting finance for HMOs can be long-winded and downright painful. I have used pretty much all of the lenders listed above and the shortest time it has taken me to re-finance an HMO is three months from the point of application to drawdown of the loan.

If you choose to use a mortgage adviser to help with the re-financing of your property, I would argue that sometimes you may not get the best product for your needs.

I once used a mortgage broker who kept trying to get me to use a specific lender. When I questioned this, and after looking at the criteria, it became apparent that this lender was the one that offered the greatest financial incentive to the broker for selling the product.

I appreciate the above comment may not apply to many financial advisers, but this practice certainly exists in a small part of the market. Therefore when I now look at taking on additional lending, I look at the following factors before choosing which mortgage company to proceed with:

- Who is the lender?
- What do they require from me in terms of experience?
- What is their exposure limit? Is there a cut-off to the number of properties you can own?
- What is the loan-to-value/purchase ratio being offered – 75% to 85%?
- What is the interest rate?
- What type of mortgage – interest-only or repayment?
- What is the arrangement fee?
- What is the application fee?
- What is the valuation fee?
- Are there any additional fees (legal/insurance)?

Here are some of the properties I have created recently where I have refinanced and pulled out all my initial costs (purchase and refurbishment costs) and have also had the opportunity to pull out additional money if required.

Case Study No 1 – Bushbury Lane, Wolverhampton

Property type (as a single let):	2-bed mid-terrace
Market value:	£60,000
Purchase price:	£40,000
Market rental:	£395pcm

As an HMO	
Converted into:	4-bed HMO
Conversion cost:	£20,000
Purchased price:	£40,000
Rental income:	£1,733pcm

	= £20,080 per annum
Valued as HMO:	£200,000
Re-finance details	
Valuation:	£200,000
70% LTV:	£140,000
Initial costs:	£60,000
Additional funds available:	£102,000

I chose to leave the additional funds in the property as equity, should I require it at a later stage.

Case Study No 2 – Westland Road, Wolverhampton

Property type (as a single let):	4-bed semi-detached
Market value:	£200,000
Purchase price:	£108,000
Market rental:	£595pcm

As an HMO

Converted into:	7-bed HMO
Conversion costs:	£50,000
Rental income:	£3,033pcm
	= £36,400 per annum
Valued as HMO:	£300,000
Re-finance details	
Valuation:	£300,000
70% LTV:	£210,000
Initial costs:	£160,000
Additional funds available:	£50,000

I chose to leave the additional funds in the property as equity, should I require it at a later stage

Case Study No 3 – Birmingham Road, West Bromwich

| Property type: | 17-bedroom care home |

Market value:	£500,000
Purchase price:	£480,000
Market rental:	£1,153pcm equivalent to £65k
	£5,415pcm

As an HMO

Converted into:	23-bed HMO
Conversion cost:	£70,000
Rental income:	£9.966pcm = £119,600 per annum
Valued as HMO:	£1,200,000

Re-finance details

Valuation:	£1,200,000
60% LTV:	£720,000
Initial costs:	£550,000
Additional funds available:	£170,000

I chose to leave the additional funds in the property as equity, should I require it at a later stage.

I hope you have seen from these examples that it is still possible to pull out all your money by creating an HMO and having it valued by a commercial surveyor on its investment value. This method has allowed me to continuously recycle my cash to increase my property portfolio year on year.

Although we are fans of the HMO strategy and have many HMOs in our portfolio, the LHA strategy can provide similar returns and is a great entry point for new investors as returns can be achieved without doing anything to, or spending money on, the properties. I think you can make a lot more money simply by working slightly smarter, and not harder, and the LHA strategy is a good case in point. As a result, our portfolio pays us very handsomely, well into six figures each year.

(A quick guide to LHA can be found in the appendix.)

We run a weekend course where we teach you all about how we set up and run our HMOs, and we will even take you on a tour around several of our properties. The course is very much geared towards the attendees on the day, depending upon whether they want to spend more time in the classroom going through the legal, financial and practical aspects of setting up and running HMOs, or whether they want to be out on the road looking at properties and seeing how it all works in practice. I think we manage a good balance, and so far all the attendees have gone away inspired and with pointers to improve their own property business. The course usually runs once a month, and if you'd like further information see the 'Come and Learn' chapter.

'You can't fall if you don't climb. But there's no joy in living your whole life on the ground.'

Unknown

Say Yes to DSS

www.dssmove.co.uk

Lesson 13: Don't judge a book by its cover

Once we were established as a letting and managing agent, and were advertising our properties in the local newspaper, we often found that people we had already turned away were still calling, week in week out. We thought we ought to expand and market more widely and so we began advertising on the major property listing portals. These are very expensive tools to use but they are market leaders in their own right so we assumed they would give us access to more potential tenants and better-quality leads.

The problem was we found that the quality of the leads was too good. Let me rephrase that. Rather than producing leads from tenants on benefits, we were mainly getting enquiries from working and professional tenants. Letting to tenants on benefits is our speciality, and of course our LHA strategy is built around that. Letting to working or professional tenants would be something of a backward step. If we went down that route then we wouldn't be able to maximise the rents using our LHA strategy, and we'd be putting the rent at 100 per cent risk again instead of only 15 per cent when we have tenants on benefits.

At that time it didn't occur to us that the popular property portals might not be the right media for us; we just assumed we weren't advertising the properties properly. So we went through all our listings and the descriptions for each property, and added a note that DSS tenants were welcome. Still nothing happened. One day, almost out of the blue, we had a telephone call from somebody who had seen one of our advertised properties, so I decided to do a bit of impromptu market research. I asked how they had found our property and they replied that they'd found it with great difficulty. The problem was that most of the listings stated no DSS. What made it more frustrating for our potential tenants was that there was no way of doing a generic search for properties that said yes to DSS. So a potential tenant could put in their search criteria and have, say, a hundred properties come up, but they'd have to go through the individual listings and descriptions of each of those hundred properties to see whether the landlord would accept DSS. It seems that most agents who advertise on the major property portals don't accept tenants on benefits, and over time many of them have given up looking for properties there. We realised that if we were going to advertise for tenants on benefits then the major property portals were not a cost-effective way for us to do so.

That got us thinking, and Aki came up with an idea. Aki, who oversees the letting agency side of the business, had done a lot of research and had discovered that on average there were one hundred thousand people on benefits looking for properties to rent in the UK, but there was no medium that offered a bespoke service. He realised that there was a major gap in the market but, being pragmatic, he really just wanted a tool that he could use to find tenants for our properties. After spending a year researching to make sure we hadn't missed any competitors, we commissioned a web development company in October 2011 to build us a bespoke property portal, and created a brand called Dssmove.co.uk.

I am proud to say that today Dssmove.co.uk is one of the only property portal for benefit-led tenancies. At the moment, and for the foreseeable future, it's free to list properties on our site. We were very keen to make our site accessible to everybody, so private landlords are welcome to list their properties as well as agents. This is the major difference between us and the other property portals, which are expensive to list with and will only accept listings from agents. Previously, private landlords were limited to using sites such as free advertising sites, but now they have access to a major nationwide niche property portal.

There may be a point in the future when we will start charging for listings, but that's still some time off. Our first goal is to make sure we become established. We are aiming to get to a critical mass of property listings where the site will become recognised as the number one portal for benefit-led tenancies, and then it will be hard to rival. As a result of our experience of letting to tenants on LHA we've made sure there are some really useful tools built in to the website that help potential tenants pre-qualify themselves.

First, we've included an LHA calculator so they can work out how much LHA they will be eligible to receive. They can then compare this figure to the quoted rent so they'll know before they contact an agent or a landlord whether they will be required to pay a top-up and how much it would be. So, if the calculator shows that they are eligible for £115 a week LHA and the rent is £525 per calendar month, or £121 a week, they know from the start that they'll need to pay a £7 a week top-up. If they can't spare £7 a week, they won't ring about that property.

> Here is how it works.
> In a year there are:
> **12 calendar months**
> **52 weeks**
> **13 x 4 weeks**
> **26 fortnights**

The second thing we did was make sure that the quoted rent is shown both weekly and per calendar month. In the world of benefits everything happens on a weekly basis, but in property, especially in the 'professional' market, everything happens per calendar month.

We decided that if we showed both figures it would eliminate a lot of confusion and miscommunication, so we made sure that everyone who lists on the site states all costs up front.

Many landlords would list a property for £400pcm and the tenant would assume this means £100 per week. In actual fact, £400pcm is £92.31 a week, so if the tenant was paying £100 a week they would be overpaying their rent. On the other hand, if the rent is £100 per week and tenant assumed that to be £400pcm, the actual rent being paid over the year would be £399.96 short (£100 per week is equivalent to £433.33 a month).

It can be extremely frustrating for the agent or landlord, and the potential tenant, to have tenants call who can't afford the property, or who can't provide a guarantor or references if they are required. So as the agent or landlord puts the details of the property on the site they have to state whether a deposit is required and how much; whether rent in advance is required and how much; whether a guarantor is required; and finally, whether there are agent's admin fees, and if so how much. If an agent or landlord advertises a property on the site and says they need a £500 deposit, £500 rent in advance and a guarantor, and that the agent's fees are £200, if the tenant hasn't got £1,200 they won't ask for more details. Putting those four fields into the system means that potential tenants are almost pre-qualified before they ring or email the agent or landlord, as long as they read the property description. This should save everyone concerned a lot of wasted time.

We've spent a small fortune on SEO (search engine optimisation) research, which means that we're ranked number one on search engines for a lot of the terms relating to benefits – LHA, DSS, Universal Credit and so on – so Dssmove.co.uk is highly visible to tenants on benefits searching on the internet. We have just had our first national letting agent come on board, who has well in excess of a hundred offices nationwide. They are uploading more and more properties every day. That's what we're after: more agents and more private landlords. We know from feedback we've received that those who've listed their properties on Dssmove.co.uk are very happy with the results, and activity on the site is building all the time. At the moment we're recording 120,000 hits per month and have 30,000 properties listed, and those numbers are growing daily.

We have the only bespoke niche site of its type, and it will be of value to anyone who is dealing with housing benefit claimants. We now have local authorities and housing associations using the site, and they are also referring benefit claimants to it to help them find accommodation. I know of landlords who have had calls from homeless charities who have found them via Dssmove.co.uk. We started it purely to resolve a problem we had: finding tenants on benefits for our properties. If you let property to tenants on benefits, or you would like to, please register on the site and upload details of your properties. Remember, it's free.

www.dssmove.co.uk

'You miss 100% of the shots you don't take.'

Wayne Gretzky

Take LHA the Easy Way

Lesson 14: Look for a solution to the problem

In February 2011, I was approached by a business acquaintance who had an idea. She wanted to set up her own payment service to help landlords collect LHA. This would operate in a similar way to the alternative banking system we were using but without the associated geographical and administrative limitations.

The reason I was so excited about her idea was because at that time we were managing properties, and were collecting LHA from ten different local authorities, including Wolverhampton, Walsall, Sandwell, Dudley, Birmingham, Telford, East Staffordshire, South Staffordshire, Cannock and Coventry.

The system we had then was that the local authority would pay the LHA payment to the tenant direct in their credit union account. The problem was that each branch operates in a slightly different way. So, for example, one area branch may pay every fortnight and may charge only £1 or £2 per transaction, whereas another area may only pay every twenty-eight days and charge up to £10 per transaction.

The idea of having a standardised payment system across our patch was very appealing. It would have been great to be involved and start it up as a joint venture, but as I am a landlord I felt there would be a clear conflict of interest. I also had to make it clear that we couldn't jeopardise our relationship with our existing provider in Wolverhampton, but we were more than happy to use the new payment services provider for our properties outside Wolverhampton. This new service, Tasker Payment Services (TPS), has been up and running since 2011 and has been a great success. One thing I really appreciate about it is that they make payment on the same day the LHA is paid, which eradicates some of the earlier issues we had.

Here, TPS outline the advantages of using their system (with consent from TPS):

Benefits

> ➢ Rent is sent to you by faster payment the same day it arrives, without delay

> ➢ Cost-effective at £4 per transaction

> ➢ Tenants no longer spend rent money on other things

> ➢ Takes away the hassle of overpayment challenges

> ➢ Overcomes Universal Credit issues

> ➢ Early warning of tenants absconding or suspensions of housing benefit

> ➢ Claims are often processed much faster

> ➢ No waiting eight weeks for direct payment

> ➢ Using TPS has been shown to result in more sustainable tenancies

> ➢ No need to use several different credit unions due to the area constraints of a common bond

How It Works In Practice

1. Tenant completes customer consent form	2. Landlord completes payee form
3. Tenant initials T&Cs	4. Provide the required ID
5. Send email to TPS to receive account details by reply within a few minutes	

We have made it a condition of our tenancy agreements that the tenant open an account with TPS, which is a very simple process and is done when the tenant comes into our office to sign their agreement. Once the account is up and running, which it should be on the day the application is received, the tenant will ask the local authority to make LHA payments into that account. LHA is paid to the landlord on the day it is received less a charge of £4 per transaction, but that's a small price to pay to achieve 100 per cent payment.

```
┌─────────────────────────────────────────┐
│                    1                      │
│  •Tenant signs tenancy agreement          │
└─────────────────────────────────────────┘
                     ↓
┌─────────────────────────────────────────┐
│                    2                      │
│  •Account set up on the same day as       │
│          application recieved             │
└─────────────────────────────────────────┘
                     ↓
┌─────────────────────────────────────────┐
│                    3                      │
│  •Tenant asks for LHA payment to be       │
│         made into TPS account             │
└─────────────────────────────────────────┘
                     ↓
┌─────────────────────────────────────────┐
│                    4                      │
│  •LHA paid to landlord on day it is       │
│    recieved minus £4 transaction fee      │
└─────────────────────────────────────────┘
```

The transaction fee of £4 is in fact less than one per cent of the rent charge, so I feel it is an appropriate amount.

This new system is built to assist landlords. Of particular importance is that if LHA is due on a particular day but isn't received, we will be notified. More often than not a zero entry suggests that there is a problem with the tenant's benefit claim. Once we are notified that payment hasn't been received we can call the tenant and find out whether there has been a problem with the

LHA itself or perhaps a problem with another of the benefits that the tenant is claiming, which has resulted in a suspension of LHA. If the tenant confirms there is problem we can invite them into the office and telephone the local authority with them, and so help the tenant to get their claim back into payment. If necessary, and with the tenant's permission, we can talk to the relevant department for them and straighten everything out. As LHA is paid fortnightly by most boroughs, we can usually get the tenant back into payment for the next payment run in two weeks' time, meaning that they will only be two weeks in arrears and will quickly catch up with their payments. Having an instant alert system like this built in helps us to keep on top of all our payments and contributes to our 100 per cent rent collection record.

And how did this person identify a need for this type of service? She realised there would be a demand when the government announced that they were bringing in Universal Credit.

If you are unfamiliar with Universal Credit and what it's all about, here's a very quick summary.:

Under the current benefits system a claimant may be eligible for, and can receive, a number of different benefits. The idea behind Universal Credit (UC) is that the government wants to replace the payment of a number of different benefits to a claimant with one single payment.

In 2012, the aim of UC was to replace:

Income-based Jobseeker's Allowance
Income-related Employment and Support Allowance
Income Support
Child Tax Credit
Working Tax Credit
Housing Benefit

The way benefits are paid will also change.

Payments will be monthly and in arrears. They will be paid into a bank account of the claimant's choosing and, because UC will include the LHA element, tenants will be expected to pay the landlord direct. Another change is that UC will be dealt with by central government and online, rather than locally in the Job Centre or the housing department of the local authority.

The government hopes to roll out UC across the country with the aim that all existing benefits claims will be switched to UC by 2017. The timescale has been put back a couple of times and it remains to be seen when it will actually be rolled out on a national basis, and when it will become the standard operating system for benefit payments.

One of the main worries that landlords have about UC is that with all credits being lumped together and made in one payment, tenants who are not used to budgeting their finances may find it difficult to budget for and pay their rent.

The beauty of using the new payment service is that if the benefit claimant elects to have their benefits paid into it they will make a note of how much of the Universal Credit is rent and will ring-fence that amount and send it to the landlord as soon as it's received. It's true that the claimant can direct them not to pay the landlord direct, but, under the terms of the account, they have to give sixty days' notice of any such change, and the landlord will be notified as soon as a request is received. This gives the landlord plenty of time to talk to the tenant and ensure that any change in their method of payment won't result in future rent arrears or problems.

The other major benefit of using this new system is that it is not limited to one geographical area and can take payments for landlords from across the whole of the country. Although Universal

Credit has not yet been brought in nationwide, I would still suggest that landlords who have tenants on benefits consider switching to the new system prior to its introduction. I say this for one very good reason, which I have mentioned earlier and from which we have benefitted on several occasions. Under the current LHA legislation if the local authority pay LHA direct to the landlord and it later transpires that they have overpaid, this can be 'clawed back' from the landlord. However, in this instance, if the tenant is being paid direct, the local authority would have to recover any monies overpaid from them.

UC is a somewhat contentious subject and I know a lot of landlords who are very fearful of its implementation. Using a payment service should reduce the risks considerably. But I think it's easy to look too much on the negative and not see the positives. One positive that landlords will be able to enjoy is that, if and when UC is introduced, they will only have to chase a single payment per property.

Let me explain what I mean. At the moment, as I have already explained, for a typical property where we charge, say, £100 per week in rent, the local authority may pay £85 of that as LHA and the tenant will pay £15 as a top-up. You will remember I said one of the attractions of having tenants on benefits is that 85 per cent of the rent is virtually risk free, and the riskiest element is the top-up, which is usually around 15 per cent.

When UC is introduced landlords will be able to tell the payment system the total rent due, and the whole amount can be ring-fenced and paid over. In fact, it is possible to arrange a similar situation today if the tenant agrees to have all of their benefits paid into an account and not just the LHA element. If they do this, the full rental amount, including the top-up, can be sent to the landlord on the day the benefits are paid into the account. So, far from being a negative, it's possible to see that its implementation, when combined with a payment service, could make the rent due 100 per cent risk free, an improvement even on the 85 per cent risk-free element that attracted me to tenants on benefits in the first place.

The only downside I can see with UC is that it is going to be paid a month in arrears. This means that ideally we will be looking to take a month's rent in advance as a deposit from all of our benefits tenants if we can, although, of course, being on benefits, many won't have it and this will reduce the number of potential tenants we are prepared to take on. When UC comes in we'll probably have to enhance our vetting and marketing procedures in order to find the very best tenants. But with a number of landlords potentially pulling out of the social rented market because of their fears over UC, and because of the generally poor way that the government treats private landlords who house social tenants nowadays, it should mean that there are more tenants to choose from for those who are still in the benefits market. If you'd like more details of this brilliant payment service and how they can help you collect your rent, go to taskerpaymentservices.co.uk.

'Build your own dreams, or someone else will hire you to build theirs.'

Farrah Gray

The Yes I Can Attitude

Lesson 15: Saying Yes opens up many more doors and opportunities.

Since the collapse of Bentley Homes and the birth of my beautiful daughter, I've completely re-evaluated what success means to me. It isn't defined now by how many properties I own or how much money I've got in the bank. I now realise that the really important things are the things you can't put a monetary value on. Being knocked down and having the ability to bounce back again has been a blessing in disguise.

But, there is one other thing that I've realised is also important, and that explains some of what has happened to me. It's my gut feelings. I often trust my gut feelings, and often they turn out right. How does that work? Maybe a gut feeling is just years of experience. In *Blink: The Power of Thinking Without Thinking* by Malcolm Gladwell reflects on this 'gut feeling.'

We live in a world that assumes that the quality of a decision is directly related to the time and effort that went into making it … We believe that we are always better off gathering as much information as possible and spending as much time as possible in deliberation. We really only trust conscious decision making. But there are moments, particularly in times of stress, when haste does not make waste, when our snap judgments and first impressions can offer a much better means of making sense of the world. The first task of Blink is to convince you of a simple fact: decisions made very quickly can be every bit as good as decisions made cautiously and deliberately

That's another good reason to get out there and try things for yourself, so that you can grow your experience and tap into those gut feelings.

I don't always get things right, and I remember a time when I ought to have listened to my gut but didn't. There used to be a pub down the road from our office, but a few years back it was demolished. After a while a 'For Sale' sign went up saying that the land was for sale with the benefit of planning consent for eight three-storey, three-bedroom houses. The asking price at that time was £400,000, which I thought was quite expensive, but, over time, slowly but surely, the price started to drop until eventually it fell to £325,000. At that price it looked quite interesting. Still, in that location I would have been happy to sit on it for a year and then sell it on for a bit more. The main problem was that we just didn't have £325,000 to spend, but, as I always try to say 'yes I can', I didn't want that to stop us from doing the deal. I started wondering whether we could get bank finance, or maybe even use bridging. So, being positive, we decided to get the deal agreed and then see if we could sort out the finance. So I called the agent and offered £325,000 with an immediate exchange of contracts and a 10 per cent deposit, but subject to completion being delayed for at least twelve months. That gave us a year to work out how to raise the £325,000.

The agent put the offer to their client, who came back and said that they would do a deal like that, but only if we paid an additional 10 per cent on the price. It was going to cost us an extra £32,500 and they wanted that extra 10 per cent upfront as part of a 20 per cent deposit.

In the end we got cold feet about it and walked away, but I kick myself now. For the sake of that extra £32,500 we could own a site that now has a massive supermarket on it who pay £90,000 a year in rent to the current owner.

We all learn from experience, and nowadays we'd do the deal and wouldn't let anyone or anything put us off. So I'm going to finish this book by telling you about a deal we've recently done where we ended up with a valuable development site just because my gut said 'go for it', and because we didn't take no for an answer. It happened like this.

Our business is based in Chapel Ash in Wolverhampton where, because it's a busy high-street location, almost all the letting agents have offices. As a child I always had to come along this street to get to Wolverhampton city centre, and I noticed there was one building that was always boarded up. Back then it was the Hop Craft Funeral Parlour. I used to say to my dad, 'Why is it boarded up?' And he would say, 'Son, no one wants it.' When I was older I would drive past and it was still boarded up. I've always known of this property and I've always had a fascination for it. Then, in September 2013, I went past and I saw two guys on ladders sticking a 'For Sale' sign on it that said it was going into a public auction on 24 October. As you can imagine, after years of watching this property I was really excited to see what would happen, but I was due to go on holiday on the day of the auction.

I said to my dad, 'You know that property that we always talk about? It's going up for sale.' He asked, 'How much?' And I said, 'I bet it's going to go for something silly. It's on a high street in a busy location in Wolverhampton.' My dad suggested that, just out of curiosity, I should call the

auctioneer to find out what price they were asking. The auctioneer said there was a guide price of £56,000 to £64,000, but I thought there's no way it's going to fetch that type of money. It looked like a decent plot of land, but I was doubtful they would get their price. I really wanted to go and have a look at it because I thought the building might be a great office for our business, but the auctioneer said they couldn't show the property because it was in such poor condition and was considered too dangerous to allow people to view. Not to be put off, I went down to have a look from the outside but I couldn't really see anything through the gates because the plot was so overgrown.

I decided to talk to my business partner and brother, Aki, and said, 'It's on for £56,000 to £64,000, but we don't know what's behind the building. We don't know how much land it's got with it or even whether the building itself is structurally sound. So we can't even know how much it's going to cost to put it right.' Aki is always the one who says, 'Well, maybe we need to think about this.' I always think in any successful business partnership you need a 'yes' man and a 'no' man. Aki is more cautious and may be the first one to say no, but will often say yes later. I'm always the 'yes' man, and I'm always looking to see if there's a deal to be had and whether we can find a way of doing it.

Undeterred, I went back to the auctioneer and asked, 'What's it going to cost to buy it outside the auction?' He said they'd already had some offers close to £80,000, but they'd all been rejected. I put in an offer of £80,000 but the auctioneer said, 'Sorry, but they've come back and said the minimum they will be prepared to accept before the auction is £100,000.' We really didn't want to spend £100,000 because we didn't know what we'd be buying, but there was something about it, and I had a gut feeling that we had to buy it. After all, I'd been watching it for fifteen years and the chances were that this property wouldn't become available again. So I said to Aki, 'We're going to offer £100,000.' He said, 'You're crazy.'

I always try to think these things through and calculate all my risks, so I wasn't suggesting we make this offer on a whim. I answered, 'Our current office costs us £15,000 a year in rent, so worst-case scenario, even if we buy the other property for £100,000, and even if we have to spend another £100,000 on it to refurbish it, it will only owe us £200,000. So compared to £15,000 in rent here, it will pay for itself in thirteen years.'

I put the offer in at £100,000 but with the proviso that it was taken out of the auction immediately. I didn't hear anything for two days and I was beginning to worry, especially as I was due to go on holiday. Then I got the call late afternoon, at four o'clock on the day before my holiday.

'Okay, Arsh, yes. We've got a deal at £100,000. It's yours as long as you can get into my office for nine o'clock tomorrow morning to sign the papers and pay the deposit.' I was meant to be flying out at seven o'clock the following morning, so I sent my wife and daughter off on the plane and delayed my flight for another day because I wanted the property so badly.

We went to the auctioneer's office and handed over a £10,000 bankers draft for the deposit and exchanged contracts, and I asked if I could have access. 'Unfortunately, no,' they replied. 'Not until you complete.' So we had already exchanged and paid the deposit and we still had no idea what we had bought.

Now I confess that what I'm about to tell you probably wasn't the right thing to do, or the right way to go about things, but I was desperate to know what we had bought. That night I got my bolt cutters out and I chopped the padlock off.

What we found was just under an acre of land behind the main office. A great result. I really had no idea about it when we made the offer. I went off on holiday to Dubai for two weeks on a real high, thinking, 'Yes! I've just done a great deal, because I'm sure we can do something with that land.' When I came back from holiday I was completely re-energised and the first thing I did was call the planning department to tell them we wanted to build houses on the land behind the office. We were keeping the office part for ourselves. The aim was to have a free office.

Despite my enthusiasm, the planning officer turned me down flat, saying, 'I'm sorry, but I don't think that land is suitable for development.' By now you will know that if someone says I can't do something I will go out of my way to make sure it happens, as I've already shown you in some of the other examples in my property journey.

It just so happens that I know the chief planning executive for Wolverhampton City Council walks past our office every day between four and a quarter past four on his way home. So after the first planning officer said no, I put a note in my diary for the next week to be in my office at that time every day. Eventually, on Thursday that week I saw the chief planner walk past so I nipped out and asked him to come in for a cup of coffee. He has a reputation of being quite difficult to see, so if you do manage to get a meeting with him you've been very fortunate. I said, 'I appreciate that you're busy but can I have five minutes of your time?' He agreed. The property I'd bought was just over the road from the office so I said, 'I've just acquired that building over the road, with all that land behind it. Can we do something together?' He said, 'Tell you what, send me an email and I'll see if I can come back to you and we'll see what we can do.'

I sent him an email that evening, and the next day he called me in for a meeting with the conservation area officer and the planning officer who had said no to me. There and then, the chief planning executive for Wolverhampton City Council said, 'I think you could put houses on the rear land.'

Originally I thought the site was big enough for three houses, but I had my architect take a look at it and together we came up with a fantastic scheme that complies with the planners' requirements, and now we've got planning consent for six houses. Six houses with an end gross development value of at least £125,000 each. So the site at the back of the property alone is worth, when built, £750,000. We had an offer only last week for the site, just for the land at the back, not including my new office, for £250,000. We are in the process of negotiating because we want a little bit more, but on the basis we can reach agreement at £300,000 we would get our £100,000 back out, and we can use the extra £200,000 to refurbish our office at the front, which means that we've got a completely free office. We decided to keep the land and apply for a second round of planning to knock down the existing eyesore and replace it with a glass-fronted contemporary building. The building would comprise offices on the ground floor and eight one-bedroom apartments on the first to third floors, making it a four-storey building. We aim to start developing in July 2015 and will either sell the apartments and houses or maintain them in the portfolio, should we see fit.

So that's my story – so far, at least. That's how Aki and I have gone from the depths of despair to getting back on our feet. As I say, I'm nothing special, and if I can do all of this in just a few years, I'm absolutely certain that you can achieve great things as well.

There are a few books I've read that you might find helpful too:

- *Rich Dad, Poor Dad* by Robert Kiyosaki
- *The Magic of Thinking Big* by David J. Schwartz
- *Who Moved My Cheese* by Spencer Johnson
- *7 Rituals of Self-Made Millionaires* by Aleksander Sinigoj
- *Outliers: The Story of Success* by Malcolm Gladwell

Reading books like these opens our eyes to the possibilities of what can happen when we control our thinking. It is a compound effect. We have one small success and we feel pleased enough to try again; we have another success and we feel much more confident … and so it goes on.

Always be ready to say 'Yes I can', and see problems as opportunities waiting to be turned around in your favour. Above all, be prepared to grab opportunities when they appear.

If there's a message I want to get across in this book, it's that things happen when you put yourself into a position for them to happen to you. Things happen when you do stuff. Opportunity seems to appear when you get out there and take action. If this can happen to me, it can also happen to you.

I also strongly believe in the principle of 'giving back' – *The Go-Giver* by Bob Burg & John David Mann is a good book to read on this subject. I've been very fortunate so I want to give back by encouraging and inspiring others, and by helping them along their property journey. And in 2011, my wife Shareen and I set up a charity, the Ellahi Charitable Foundation, as a means of supporting the education of children in one of the poorest slums in Southeast Asia. Mr Mohammed Gulzar Kaliqi had a vision to make a difference to the lives of the people in this area and opened a school in 2000, but when he passed away in 2010 the school building was only partially completed. We decided to help make his dream come true and raise the funds to finish the building. We are well on our way but we require a little more funding to complete this project. If you feel you could assist with any part of this effort, please visit

www.e-c-f.co.uk

'Life isn't about getting and having, it's about giving and being.'

Kevin Kruse

Would You Like to Work With Me?

Lesson 16: Make sure you are always educating and bettering yourself

I'm looking for a number of commercially astute people to come into business with us.

Rent-me-now has been established for over five years, and in January 2014 we launched our franchise model. On the strength of the figures and turnover we have generated in our Wolverhampton property management and lettings business, we found our first franchisee within just a couple of weeks. We are now helping them to build their own similar, high-turnover, high-profit business.

We are looking to work with twenty new franchisees, each with their own geographic area, every year for the next three years. A franchisee will be able to trade using the Rent-me-now brand and logo and have full access to the systems, strategies and techniques that we've developed, some of which have been detailed in this book.

Each franchisee will get full training. We will show you in detail how a standard property, which may let for £500 a month, could potentially earn a commission of up to £850 per month. A traditional letting agent or managing agent might only receive a fee of £50 plus VAT per property per month.

Where an agency using the traditional model may earn 10 per cent, the Rent-me-now model produces an average commission of around 25 to 30 per cent, with a minimum monthly commission of £100 per property. One of the beauties of the Rent-me-now model is that it is essentially recession-proof because it is all benefits driven. This strategy can be replicated in any town or city in the country.

The potential returns from using our strategies and techniques are astounding. Just think of this: if you're able to generate £850 per month from a property that would normally rent for £500 per month, you'll be making seventeen times more than a traditional letting agent.

Using this example, you could easily generate commission of £10,200 per year just from one property, which means you will be making more money from the property than if you actually owned it. And, of course, there will be other potential income streams as well. For instance, you could charge administration fees to landlords and tenants, although the 'head office' model in Wolverhampton doesn't do this because we don't want to create a barrier to entry for either landlord or tenant. But you could legitimately assist landlords with arranging maintenance and charge for the service.

You will also be able to position yourself with landlords so that you can have first right of refusal to buy a property if they wish to sell, or you could negotiate rent-to-rent deals with them (if you're not sure what this is, don't worry; we'll explain all of this at our training), or could even control their properties by way of lease options (again, if you're not sure what this involves we will train you in all aspects). You can also use these techniques to build your own personal private property portfolio.

In our business, many of the competing franchises won't allow their franchisees to build their own private property business in the background, but we are of the opinion that it's an advantage if our franchisees are active property investors. We will not only encourage you, we will help you wherever we can. Franchise fees will vary depending upon the region, but will typically be between £15,000 and £25,000.

But what if you don't have £15,000 or £25,000 to start your business? Well, as an alternative to the franchise model Rent-me-now are prepared to undertake a joint venture (JV) with a suitable partner or partners. Rather than paying a franchise fee we would expect a JV partner to put up working capital of £10,000, which we will then match. JV partners will also need to commit to stay in the business for a minimum of three years.

As a JV partner we will invite you to come and work with us at our headquarters in Wolverhampton and spend at least twenty days with us in the office, learning the systems and being involved in the day-to-day running of the strategies and techniques. By being hands-on like this, under our supervision and guidance you will learn how to implement the LHA and other strategies so you can hit the ground running when you return to your own patch.

As a JV partner you will also benefit from the creation of a 'central hub', which means that once you put an LHA claim in to your local council, 'HQ' in Wolverhampton will be able to track all your claims and take payments for you. This means that HQ can then pay landlord clients for you, giving you more time to go out and build the business, and so relieve you of a lot of the time-consuming administration. JVs will be run on a true and full 50/50 basis so you can be assured that it's in our interest to see you succeed and to help you do so.

Whether you become a franchisee or a JV partner, we are fully committed to you and your success. We will be with you every step of the way, training you, advising you and assisting you to build your business. The Rent-me-now brand name is important to us and we are not going to allow our JV partners or franchisees to do anything but succeed.

The figures we have achieved in Wolverhampton from the three hundred properties we manage produce commissions and profit equivalent to managing over a thousand properties the traditional way. For us it's all about working smarter, not harder.

We hold regular open days at our offices in Wolverhampton where we explain both of these business opportunities in detail.

If you'd like more details, please do get in touch. We are looking forward to talking to you.

arsh.ellahi@rent-me-now.co.uk

'Remember no one can make you feel inferior without your consent.'

Eleanor Roosevelt

Come and Learn

Lesson 17: Always, always take the opportunity to learn

Every month I run concise training courses on a range of topics that have been introduced in the book. The courses are a way of networking with other property professionals as well as gaining an in-depth knowledge of how I manage and run all the systems I have discussed.

The courses are suitable for everyone from novice investors to seasoned multi-portfolio landlords who are looking to gain knowledge in a relaxed and informal manner. I encourage an interactive atmosphere, and delegates are encouraged to ask questions and participate in discussions throughout. Course materials and resources are available, along with follow-on support after the course.

Alongside me, I have a number of specialists who provide a wealth of information about various aspects of property, from architect support for HMOs to tax and HMO finance specialists, who are on hand to offer support and guidance.

Two high-cash-generating strategies are explored in great detail with real working examples during the course; these strategies are proven to work nationwide. Previous delegates have gone on to implement the strategies the very next day and have increased their cash flow from their existing portfolio almost immediately with no further investment.

Setting Up HMOs

Course Content

'The Ultimate HMO Tour'
Four HMOs with
£200,000 rental income

Analysis of every aspect
of the property and
systems in place

A step-by-step guide to
appropriate legislation in
your area and how to
apply

Legalities and fire safety
regulations in HMOs

Structuring HMOs so
tenants are responsible
for their own utility bills

Finance masterclass

Making LHA Work For You

Course Content

Generating greater cash
flow from your single-let
properties

Introduction to the
benefits market and how
it works

Understanding tenant
psychology and how to
deal with them

Tricks and tips for dealing
with everyday issues

Understanding housing
benefit applications and
getting them right

Legal rights and
responsibilities

Tenant interview
techniques

As well as these courses, I work with a variety of well-known speakers who are specialists in their fields. These course are run throughout the UK and offer an intensive approach to rent-to-rent and deal-sourcing strategies.

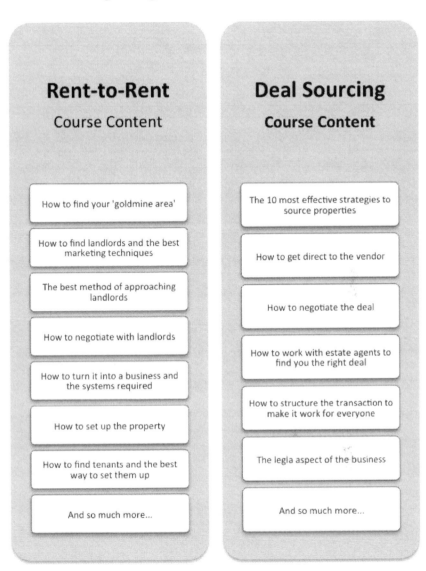

I'm always especially excited when I hear that previous course attendees have used the information they learnt and made a profit from it. Here is an example of the success a course attendee has experienced in a relatively short space of time.

A guy from Liverpool attended one of our courses in 2013 and rang me for some advice about a property he owns. It's a two-bedroom mid-terrace property he bought for £60,000. He was about to rent the property to a family, but he called me to make sure he had set the deal up the right way. I am always happy to speak to any of our course delegates, and we worked out the figures together. We calculated he could generate £220 a week from this property, which is just short of £11,500 a year. That means on his £60,000 purchase price he is generating a yield of 19 per cent.

He didn't have to create an HMO to achieve this yield and the property hasn't been changed physically in any shape or form. He simply houses a family on benefits and applied the information he had learnt on the course.

If you'd like to attend our course and learn how to structure tenancies like this, it would be great to see you. We teach you how to buy a property and how to get it to generate high cash flow using our LHA strategy without doing any additional work to the property. We show you how to find the right tenants, how to structure the tenancies and how to liaise with the local authority to make sure you get paid the maximum possible amount.

To find out more about the course content and the location of your nearest course, please see www.arshellahi.com.

Contacts

www.arshellahi.com

www.rent-me-now.co.uk

www.dssmove.co.uk

www.webuypropertiesfast.co.uk

www.e-c-f.co.uk

APPENDIX

Quick Guide to LHA

In April 2008 Housing Benefit was replaced by the Local Housing Allowance (LHA).

The amount of LHA a claimant will receive is calculated taking into account the rental values of properties in the area and the number of bedrooms needed by the claimant. A consequence of this is that the amount a claimant is entitled to may be more or less than the actual asking rent of the property. When a claimant applies for LHA, they will be assessed as needing a bedroom for each of the following people in their household:

- An adult couple
- Another person aged 16 or over
- Any two children of the same sex up to the age of 16
- Any two children regardless of sex under the age of 10
- Any other child

There is a maximum weekly rate of LHA based on the number of bedrooms a household qualifies for. The maximum amounts payable in the UK are:

- £250 for a one-bedroom property
- £290 for a two-bedroom property
- £340 for a three-bedroom property
- £400 for a four-bedroom property

However, the amount of LHA a claimant receives will depend on where they live. Local limits are based on the cheapest 30 per cent of properties in an area and vary widely across the UK.

In Wolverhampton, for example, the current rates are:

- £60 shared room rate
- £86.54 for a one-bedroom property
- £106.13 for a two-bedroom property
- £117.92 for a three-bedroom property
- £150 for a four-bedroom property

The maximum amount receivable is limited to the top rate in the local area for a four-bedroom property. A claimant can still rent a larger home, but will only get LHA up to the maximum level for four bedrooms. This means it's likely that the LHA won't cover all the rent if they occupy a larger and/or more expensive property.

If a claimant is under the age of thirty-five or is occupying shared accommodation, they are usually only entitled to LHA at the shared accommodation rate regardless of

the size of the property they rent. This is lower than the rate for a one-bedroom property. This applies even if they can't find shared accommodation in their area and are renting a property on their own. So, if a claimant is under the age of thirty-five and rents a one-bedroom flat they will still only receive the shared rate and not the one-bedroom rate. Where the tenant's circumstances means that the LHA they will receive doesn't cover the rent for a property, a landlord will have to decide whether to accept that claimant as a tenant, whether to reduce the rent they are seeking so that the claimant can take the property, or whether to require the claimant to pay a 'top-up', in other words pay the balance outstanding between the LHA they receive and the rent.

LHA is usually paid directly to the person who claims it, and that person is expected to pay the rent to the landlord. However, the council must make LHA payments direct to the landlord if:

- The claimant has rent arrears of eight weeks or more
- It is already making deductions from their Income Support, Jobseeker's Allowance or Employment Support Allowance to pay for rent arrears

In some circumstances, the council can, at its own discretion, choose to pay the LHA direct to the landlord. It might do this if:

for example if they have problems with drugs or alcohol, or they have a serious medical condition

- They are unlikely to pay their rent, for example if the council is aware they have consistently failed to pay the rent in the past

Councils also have the right to pay LHA direct to a landlord if it will help the claimant to get a tenancy or keep an existing tenancy, for example:

- For existing tenants – if the rent has been reduced to an affordable level (which is normally the LHA rate for the property)
- For new tenants – if the rent has been reduced to an affordable level or direct payments will help a tenant keep their tenancy

Printed in Great Britain
by Amazon